Refuge

Leah Everly

DEDICATION

This book is dedicated to my husband and children – the best people I could ever ask to share my life with.

CONTENTS

INTRODUCTION

Let the peace of Christ rule in your hearts,
since as members of one body you were called to peace.
And be thankful.
Colossians 3:15

I still remember the first time I saw my husband in his uniform. It had taken years to get to that point, and I was so ridiculously proud of him. Proud enough that even though his first day of work started before the crack of dawn, I followed him out the door and made him stop to pose for a picture. He humored me, even though it made him feel like a kid going to kindergarten for the first time. I then went back to bed, but was way too excited to sleep.

Even though I was excited, I was also struck with a healthy dose of fear that day as his dreams became reality. I knew his crisp new uniform would demand a lot from him. I realized he was going to be in physical danger all day, every day, from that point forward. I realized he now had a target on his back by police haters. I knew that even though his new uniform carried a lot of respect, there were also a lot of people who would hate him simply because of it, no matter who he was as a person. I was only a few weeks pregnant at the time, and even though I tried not to dwell on it, the thought of being a widowed mom wasn't far from my mind.

As a police wife reading this, I'm sure you can relate. Whether you met your husband when he was already in law enforcement or went through the recruitment and hiring process as a couple, the danger of the job is no doubt on your mind, maybe more than you'd like it to be. I know from the moment my husband first told me he wanted to be a police officer, I had my concerns. While I got used to some of them over time, new fears undoubtedly came as I learned more about what this life meant; as I learned more about the specific kinds of dangers he would face.

This is especially true when I realized the dangers faced by law enforcement officers don't end with the threat of physical injury, but also extend to his mental well-being, and, as a result, to his most important relationships. One of the things my husband was most consistently told in the academy (besides "watch the hands") was that this job is associated with a high divorce rate – something like 80%.

Even though the idea of that high of a divorce rate was scary, that particular danger had one big benefit: it was something I did have a little control over. As a recovering control freak, I wanted more than anything to take that small measure of control and run with it. I decided I would do what I could to protect him, our marriage, and our family from the negative effects of law enforcement as much as I could. I wanted to leave as little of that up to chance as possible.

I knew there would be situations I wouldn't be able to fix. I knew there would be things he wouldn't want to talk about and pain I wouldn't be able to take away. What I could do, however, was make sure that our home was a safe place for him to fall apart. While he served and protected society, I could serve and protect our home. I wanted to do everything I could to make our home a place of peace and safety – a refuge from the storm.

Over the past few years, my commitment has been tried and tested again and again through a hiatus in his long-awaited law enforcement career, a severe decline in his physical health, financial crises, and other personal challenges. Through it all, we've learned to come together as a couple and be stronger than ever – because I knew that a peaceful, loving, safe home needed to be a priority, no matter what.

The truth is, life is hard. Full stop. No matter what job you or your husband hold, no matter what challenges you specifically face, life is just hard. Law enforcement absolutely has the potential to make it that much harder, making a peaceful home that much more difficult to establish. However, because law enforcement can make your life harder, that makes transforming your home into a refuge that much more important.

When the storms are stronger, it's that much more powerful to have people who love and support you. Having a place where you can feel loved, respected, and able to fall apart without judgment makes everything else a little easier to deal with. It makes every challenge a little less bitter, every trial a little less trying. It will enable everyone you interact with to do what they're called to do a little better, because they will have the emotional support they need.

To make your home a true refuge, you have to start with you. Making changes to your dwelling has to start with making you different from the inside out – that means becoming happier, more peaceful, and better able to partner with God through all the trials. That's where this devotional starts, because without this crucial first step, nothing else will fall into place. That's not to say you have to be perfect, not by any means. It's all about identifying a few key habits that will help you be more fulfilled and better able to support your family through everything.

Next, this book will focus on having a more peaceful marriage. This is the next most important thing to focus on because you and your spouse are the leaders of your home. It's important that you're on the same page for the sake of both of you, plus your kids. It means a lot less confusion for them, and a lot more harmony for everyone.

A good marriage is at the root of a strong family — a family which can then go forth and change the world Being able to divorce-proof your marriage, making it one your kids can depend on and look up to, gives your kids a better chance of having healthy relationships of their own in the future. The strength of your home can have a long-reaching impact on those around you, even beyond those who live in the four walls of your home: strengthening, inspiring, and uplifting simply by being a good example.

Next, we'll talk about how to find greater peace in your parenting. This can be a daunting task, especially when you spend a lot of time solo parenting, but I'm here to encourage you that it's not impossible. Not at all! It takes a little change in mindset, the acknowledgement that you can't (and don't need to) to it all, and a lot of help from your Father in Heaven. You can have a peaceful home with children, whether you're currently in the midst of toddler temper tantrums or full-on teenage rebellion.

Lastly, we'll combine all these aspects in the final section by addressing the spirit of your home. After all, you, your marriage, and your parenting style don't exactly exist in a vacuum. Each of these relationships impacts the others, for better or worse. Recognizing that and doing what you can to ensure harmony between them is an important step to making your home a refuge.

The greatest thing about all of these tasks is that you can partner with God in your efforts — and that's exactly what this devotional sets out to do. You'll be guided through scriptures to become more familiar with God's promises to you and how He wants you to care for your family. You'll connect with Him on a deeper level as you strive to guide your family to peace.

Building up your home as a refuge for your family is possibly the most powerful thing you could do, and I'm so happy you've joined me in this journey.

If you want to make the most of this devotional, here are my suggestions of what you should have with you as you read:

- A journal for your thoughts (unless you'd prefer to write in this book – and if that's the case, go for it! It's your book, do what you want with it!)

- A Bible (physical or digital) so you can look up relevant scriptures and delve deeper into His word as the spirit prompts you.

- A growth mindset and openness to change.

Most of all, I want to encourage you that no matter what your home life looks like at present, there's always hope to make it better. I love the verse in Proverbs 24:16: "For though the righteous fall seven times, they rise again; but the wicked stumble when calamity strikes." You don't have to be perfect to be righteous – you just have to be willing to try again.

For any family, having a home that is a place of refuge is powerful, but when your husband faces the worst the world has to offer, it's that much more important. It has that much more capability to change the world for the better.

I'm so excited to delve into this devotional with you, and I can't wait to see what you do with it.

PEACEFUL YOU

You will keep in perfect peace those whose minds are steadfast,
because they trust in you.
Isaiah 26:3

About a week before my daughter was born, I had a complete meltdown at church. My son was being so incredibly defiant, but weirdly needy at the same time. It was partially because of his age, but also because he knew he had a very short time left as an only child and it was freaking him out. Understandable, sure, but still trying. Naturally, it was also a week where my husband was largely incommunicado, so I felt like I was all alone as a parent.

On top of that, our tiny apartment was an absolute mess. It was cluttered beyond what my "nesting instincts" could take, if that gives you any idea. I'd clean for an hour, then cry because it didn't seem to look any different. It seemed more like the junk had just been rearranged. I had panicked visions of the baby choking on the LEGO pieces my son refused to clean up, and freaked out accordingly. I had no idea how I was going to find the time to clean and organize the place enough that I felt comfortable bringing a baby home.

So with all that lingering on my mind, I had very little patience when my son decided to completely lose it during the church service. I picked him up in a huff and brought him out into the hall with the intention of talking to him. Instead, I put him on a chair next to me and bawled my eyes out. I'd hit my limit and I didn't even have the energy to scold him anymore.

One of the sweet ladies at church walked over, quietly sat next to me, and asked what she could do to help. I sobbed harder and dumped all my problems on her. Poor lady. Bless her heart for listening as I ranted about everything that was bothering me. At the end of my tirade, her response really struck me.

She said, "I hear that you're taking care of everything and everyone, but who's taking care of you?"

I had honestly never thought of that before. I was so focused on getting things in order and making sure my family was happy that I neglected to think about my own needs. I was doing nothing to make sure they were being met. I mean, I *saw* my needs and was frustrated I couldn't get what I needed, but that was the extent of it.

Any chance that sounds familiar?

With your husband in law enforcement, you have tons of responsibilities on your plate. You're there for your husband when he's misplaced part of his uniform (at 5 AM). You're there for your kids as they cope with the unpredictability of Daddy's schedule — you know, in between helping them with their homework. You help referee fights between the kids and even sometimes between your kids and your husband because they're not quite connecting, and you and you alone know how to close to gap.

You have a lot to take care of, no doubt. You have so much on your plate, and truthfully, you don't have a lot of spare time. It's easy to let self-care slide to the backburner in the midst of survival mode. It's not necessarily an absolute "must-do", after all, so it's easy to let it slide in favor of more pressing issues. Wash, rinse, and repeat, and you're bound for complete burnout.

The fact is, though, that if you want to continue being an awesome mom and wife, you're going to have to find a way to sustain yourself. Being awesome at those things requires a lot of energy, both emotional and physical. If you don't take the time to refill your energy reserves, you won't be able to keep up with the demands of your family.

Or, well, you might be able to, but not without breakdowns in church hallways to sweet old ladies who are too nice to back away slowly.

If you want to be the best mom and wife you can be, you need to know who you can turn to in times of need, both spiritually and temporally. You need to find confidence in the woman God made you to be. You also need to figure out ways to give yourself grace to be wonderfully imperfect as you do your best to accomplish everything you've been called to do.

As such, this chapter is all about how you can do all those things. Because as amazing as you are, you're just one person! One wonderful, caring, talented person who deserves to be taken care of, too. So let's start making sure your needs are met – because you deserve it, and also because it will help you be there for your family the best way you can.

SECTIONS

- Where Can You Turn For Peace?
- You're The Best You
- Reasonable Expectations
- Make The Most Of Your Time

WHERE CAN YOU TURN FOR PEACE?

Come to me, all ye heavy laden; and I will give you rest.
Matthew 11:28

Sometimes, it just seems like everything hits all at once. There was a week recently where my son and daughter apparently hit a simultaneous growth spurt, complete with the requisite moaning and groaning. As if that wasn't enough, my husband went out of town during this time, then got sick, then, as soon as he got better, went right back to work, with his own moaning and groaning when he arrived back home.

It seemed like everyone was melting down around me. Everyone needed something from me, all at the same time. If it wasn't my daughter needing to nurse, it was my son demanding a steady stream of Curious George and fruit snacks. My husband needed an ice pack and some caffeine because he had a migraine, which meant he got frustrated with the kids when they wouldn't quiet down. I ended up having to soothe some frayed nerves over that, too; both my husband's and my kids'.

In the meantime, the housekeeping world kept spinning with its own responsibilities. It's the neverending story of adulthood, isn't it? Even though I gave up mid-week and started using paper plates, we couldn't exactly stick to paper clothes or bath towels or anything. Basic maintenance doesn't feel quite so basic when you're already completely tapped out. It becomes just another slog.

I'll tell you one thing for sure. Keeping your cool when everyone seems to be melting down around you is not easy. You know what is easy? Gaining 10 pounds in a week from stress eating. I'm speaking from experience on that one for sure. Not losing your mind? Not quite so easy.

I spent the first half of the week feeling so overwhelmed I just wanted to curl up in a ball and cry while the world caved in around me. After a couple days, I knew something had to change. I did the only thing I could think to do: pray. And as I did so, God brought to mind all the scriptures that promise God is there in all the overwhelm – classics like:

> "So do not fear, for I am with you; do not be dismayed, for I am your God. I will strengthen you and help you; I will uphold you with my righteous right hand."
>> - Isaiah 41:10

> "I can do all things through Christ who gives me strength."
>> - Phillippians 4:13

> "God is our refuge and strength, an ever-present help in trouble. Therefore we will not fear, though the earth give way and the mountains fall into the heart of the sea, though its waters roar and foam and the mountains quake with their surging."
>> - Psalm 46:1-3

Every time you don't feel capable of meeting the needs of those around you, remember that you serve a God who is capable. Forget how incompetent you feel, because you don't have to be strong enough right now. Instead, focus on what amazing things God is capable of –

because He is the one who is going to get you through it, moment by moment.

Think of it this way: If Christ can heal a leper, he can renew your patience for your family when they're being completely unreasonable and your nerves are feeling frayed. If the power of God can let Moses part the Red Sea, surely that same power can give you the energy you need to care for your husband and kids even when the baby has kept you up all night and you're running on a cumulative two hours of sleep.

If God can make a mountain move with just a little faith, why shouldn't you think He can move your mountain of responsibilities and clear your path to peace? Even if He chooses not to remove those responsibilities, He can help you re-center, figure out where to start, and take things one by one. He can even advise you on what things can be let go of completely.

On those nights where nobody sleeps, on those days that are long and full of nonstop drama, in those moments that you, too, just want to throw yourself on the ground and scream, you have to realize something. God is there. He is always willing to help you, just as He always has, and will help you get through it. He can help you make the right decisions for yourself and your family, no matter how daunting each moment becomes.

After all, you worship the God of Abraham and Isaac. Of Moses, who stood before the Red Sea with the pharoah's armies rapidly approaching. Of Daniel, who survived the lion's den. Of David, who took out the giant with just a sling and a stone. That same God can undoubtedly help you face the pressures of being a law enforcement wife.

When you compare those huge miracles to the struggles you're facing, your problems will start to feel a lot smaller and more manageable. If you move forward with faith, looking at the amazing things He has done before, you will undoubtedly start to believe He can work miracles in your life, too.

As you work to be a place of peace for your family, remember that He is your most reliable source of peace. No matter how lonely you feel, He's there to be with you. No matter what emotional load you're carrying for your husband, He's there to pick up the other side and help you out. No matter what headstrong child is challenging you right now, He sees it and will provide you what you need to meet the challenge head-on with love and grace.

With that in mind, how can you more readily access this power? Truthfully, it comes down to depending on Him first and foremost, instead of on your own power and abilities. It starts by admitting that you can't do it alone, but trust that He can help you do it. A humble, faithful, teachable heart is what He needs to accomplish miracles.

In your everyday life, it's also important to make time to feed your relationship with God, even in small ways. Small, persistent effort to do things like pray, study scriptures, and serve others can help you feel closer to Him and recognize His promptings more clearly.

Undoubtedly, as you draw nearer to God, He will likewise draw near to you. As you seek Him, you'll be better able to find Him. The more you obey what He asks you to do, the more direction He will give you.

Never lose sight of the fact that He is your greatest advocate in this life. He is the one who perfectly understands you, who loves you absolutely, and will never, ever let you down. Even when it feels like He has abandoned you (as we all feel at times!), I guarantee He is just around the corner with the answers you so desperately seek.

Every day, remember to lean into Him. Get on your knees and pray, then move forward confidently to do what you're called to do –

because He made you just for this purpose, and will give you the peace you need to make it happen.

PRAYER IDEAS

- Express gratitude for God's promises of help, hope, rest, and comfort in every circumstance.
- Pray for peace in a your current trials.
- Pray for rest when your heart can't take any more.
- Pray for discernment when trying to make a decision – even if it seems minor to you, He will help you with it.
- Pray to see His hand in everything around you, especially your struggles.
- Pray to know the next steps you need to take when you're too overwhelmed to even start.

YOU'RE THE BEST YOU

There are different kinds of gifts, but the same Spirit distributes them.
1 Corinthians 12:4

I have to admit that before I had my first child, I was absolutely terrified of becoming a mother. I wanted children, don't get me wrong. My heart fluttered when thinking about a baby of our own, but I also had serious doubts about my ability to love and nurture my child properly. Even after I worked at a daycare (and loved it!), the 24/7-ness of motherhood seemed daunting because I've never considered myself a "kid person."

For instance, one of my least favorite things is when Christmas songs on the radio use choirs of kids in the middle. I find it super annoying and schmaltzy. In fact, that's still the case. My dirty secret is when I was considering enrolling my son in preschool, I ruled one out solely because they had regular singing recitals. I didn't think I could grin and bear it that often. Luckily my son isn't into that kind of thing anyway, so I may have saved both of us.

Over time, I've come to realize that those shortcomings don't actually matter. They don't make me a bad mom. They just make me different, and that's okay. For instance, I don't know a lot of nursery rhymes. When my son was crying inconsolably as a baby, I ended up just singing him whatever was stuck in my head at the time (even Bon Jovi's *You Give Love A Bad Name* – true story). He loved it just the same, because the song was being sung by his loving mom He still felt my love and got the affection he needed, just not in the way you might see in a Hallmark movie. He's got pretty good taste in music as a result, so that's good.

In any case, my ability to parent is definitely not the only thing in my life that's made me ask, "Am I really good enough?" I personally suffer from severe case of "never-good-enough-itis". I'm constantly wondering whether I'm doing enough, being enough, or generally if I'm enough for anybody. I can name an endless number of situations in which I felt insecure about myself, wondering why I wasn't better at something.

If I'm being honest, I've felt that way about every aspect of my life before, and I wouldn't be surprised if you have, too. It's easy to scroll through Instagram and see beautiful representations of other people's lives and start wondering, "Why can't I be more like them?" Whether it's the mom who makes Pinterest-worthy crafts with her kids all the time, the wife who always goes on lavish vacations with her husband (especially if they're kid-free), or the woman who posts #fitspo photos that make you feel frumpy.

It's easy to feel unsure of yourself when you start comparing your entire wonderfully imperfect self to the carefully staged, filtered, and Photoshopped achievements of others. When you see others succeed and you see the apparent happiness that comes with that success, it's normal to start questioning your value, your abilities, and generally your own awesomeness.

The thing is, nobody else's achievements actually detract from the awesome things about you. When you keep your eyes on your own paper, so to speak, you can better recognize that the things that make you different from others are exactly what make you so perfectly suited to your own family. That means it doesn't matter if you're good at whatever another woman is good at – you can just focus on being competent at the things that are specifically important to those in your life.

The things you're not so good at but would like to be better at? You can absolutely spend time developing them. It's your prerogative – you can practice and improve over time, and that's an awesome capability. On the other hand, it's also okay to recognize that there are things you're not good at and accept them as they are. You don't have to be Super Woman and be able to do everything 100% perfectly, all the time. Take comfort in the fact that nobody is!

The fact is, the gifts God has given you are different from those He has given to others. It's true. And it's okay! He gave them to you with a purpose. He knew what you would face in your life. He knew what you would need, and He gave you exactly the tools you would need to do those things. He knows who you are, and you are capable of doing everything He has asked you to do. The gifts God has given you are specifically for that purpose.

I know I find that the more time I spend magnifying the gifts God has given me rather than wishing for others, the happier I am. If I spend time comparing, complaining, and griping because I'm not as good at something else as someone else is, I'm not nearly as happy, because I'm focused on the wrong things. It's hard to be happy when you focus on what you don't have!

You don't have to be anybody but yourself to be the best mother and wife possible for your family. You're married to your husband for a reason. You were given your children for a reason. God knew what He was doing when he gave you your life, your personality, and your gifts, so take comfort in that.

What's most important to remember is that every single gift is a gift from God. Whether that gift is a natural knack for dealing with children, singing beautifully, being a whiz at math, or heck, something like being super good at flower arranging, make sure to use it to glorify God. If you do that, He will help you magnify those gifts and use them to make the world a much better place.

PRAYER IDEAS

- Express gratitude for the gifts God has given you.
- Thank God for the opportunities He has given you to develop those gifts.
- Pray for the eyes to be able to recognize your gifts and how they benefit you, your family, and everyone around you.
- Pray to focus on what you are good at and stop comparing yourself to others.
- Pray to show yourself grace for your imperfections, and pray for assistance as you work to improve.

REASONABLE EXPECTATIONS

But seek first the kingdom of God and his righteousness,
and all these things will be added to you.
Matthew 6:33

I heard this idea once. I don't remember what it was called. Maybe just the "choose two" principle. Whatever the name, it was the idea that as a mom and wife, of the following list, you can only choose two at any given moment:

- Clean house
- Full-time job
- Healthy dinners
- Extra time with kids
- Fit and toned body
- Thriving love life
- Full night's sleep
- Homemade anything

But, of course, as the control freak and perfectionist I can be the thought made me sad. I thought, I have to be able to choose more than just two. I mean really, just two? Of all those? I have a chronic case of "shiny object syndrome" that makes it hard to focus on a specific task at any given time.

Just ask my husband, and he can attest that I have the tendency to get irrationally excited about new possibilities – excited enough that I get tempted to drop everything I'm currently working on and run with the Brand New Thing, no matter how ill-advised. It's kind of a problem.

At the same time, I don't want to be considered flaky. I'm supposed to be able to do everything, right? My solution is to just add that New Thing to my running list of old exciting things, rather than re-prioritizing my schedule. And hoo-boy, I exhaust myself really quickly trying to make all that happen.

I've struggled against myself for years, wanting to do all the things, be everything for everyone, and be fantastically amazing at everything I tried. The issue with not being able to do it all wasn't, in fact, my inability to do it all. It was my attitude toward myself for having normal, human limitations.

This became even more glaringly apparent when I first became a mom at the same time my husband had his super demanding week on/week off, 12 hour shift schedule which rotated from days to nights every six weeks. I was convinced if I just tried hard enough, I could do all the things. I could have a happy baby, a clean house, healthy meals, and I could even lose the baby weight in a snap — and, on top of it all, be totally emotionally stable.

Obviously, it wasn't possible. The harder I tried, the more I had myself convinced that it wasn't a matter of it not being possible. It was because I just wasn't good enough. I just had to push farther, work harder, and I could make the things happen. If I'm being honest, I'm slightly addicted to the feeling of accomplishment.

The reality of the sheer lack of time to commit to #allthethings didn't actually click until relatively recently. Like, the last few months, if I'm being honest — though it may just be a lifelong struggle. I caught myself falling back into the same trap recently and literally had to write at the top of my planner, "Keep it simple! It's okay to just survive.

You don't have to be supermom." The last part was underlined three times, because I knew I would ignore my own advice later.

In this day and age, it can be really hard to be comfortable with who you are, as you are. When you see all the possibilities out there, feeling comfortable just rocking the basics can make you feel deficient somehow. Even if you're not a hardcore shiny object syndrome sufferer, there are lots of super shiny, awesome things around that can lure even the most focused person away from what they are truly called to do.

Those things can be awesome, not going to lie! The newest workout program. A new way to learn a language. A super-awesome curriculum for math or science or reading with your kids. Even a new job. Surely you see the same exciting ads for new things on Facebook when you scroll through that I do, right?

The thing is, God hasn't called you to do all the things. God has called you to do a set of particular things based on your particular skills, or lack thereof. He doesn't want you to do everything, because you can't! You don't have time. It's not in your abilities as a mortal. And He doesn't need you to do that. What a relief.

When it comes down to it, what's most important? The things that are most important are the things that last the longest – things like your relationships with your husband and kids. And, of course, your relationship with God. Apart from those, what you are called to do is so individualized you'll have to rely on God to determine that. One person might be called to be a working mom. Another might be called to stay at home. Some may be called to homeschool while others are not.

Having reasonable expectations for yourself means realizing the only important things are the things God has asked you to do. He doesn't ask you to do things to the extreme. He just wants you to do them to the best of your ability. If that means being average, there's nothing wrong with that.

Showing yourself grace means realizing you don't have to be super woman. You don't have to be the perfect wife or mom to be exactly what your family needs — or exactly what God needs you to be. You are worth so much more than your limitations.

Be willing to treat yourself like you would someone you really love. Build yourself up. Talk to yourself nicely. Take care of yourself. See yourself through God's eyes, trusting that He knows who you have the potential to become and will help you get there. Trust that He will never leave your side as you pick yourself up off the ground after every fall and try again. Know that He will never give up on you, so don't give up on yourself!

When you struggle with this, feel free to pray to see yourself, even momentarily, as He sees you. I promise it will be an eye opening experience — it sure was when I did just that. I saw myself as someone worthwhile, someone who could do anything she set her mind to, someone who had unlimited potential and would be lifted up at the last day if I continued to try and do the things the Lord wanted me to do. It was unbelievable. Because I definitely haven't seen myself that way before that day!

Show yourself grace, because beating yourself up about every mistake isn't going to help you. It's not going to help you get where you want to be. It will distract you so much that you'll find it hard to be a light for Christ in this dark world, which is so desperately needed.

God knows the truth about who you are. He knows your strengths, your weaknesses, your desires, your fears, and everything you're capable of. His is the only opinion that truly matters. When in doubt, look to what He has to say about you and nobody else.

When it comes right down to it, you can't do everything, and nobody is expecting you to. When you focus on the things that matter most, Heavenly Father will help everything else fall exactly where they're supposed to be.

PRAYER IDEAS

- Express gratitude for the knowledge that you don't have to do everything – that what you can do is enough for Him, and for your family.
- Pray for help prioritizing your to-do list when it feels overwhelming.
- Pray for help discerning the decisions that are best for you and your family.
- Pray for the eyes to see yourself as He does so that you can feel encouraged by His love.
- Pray for help forgiving yourself when you get sidetracked from the work He needs you to do

MAKE THE MOST OF YOUR TIME

*Be very careful, then, how you live — not as unwise but as wise,
making the most of every opportunity because the days are evil.
Therefore do not be foolish but understand what the Lord's will is.
Ephesians 5:15-17*

I have a confession for you. Every few months, I get slightly addicted to a game on my phone. It's a different one every time, but without fail, I find something new to obsess over and waste my time on. It starts out small, but then I find myself spending more and more time each day until I realize it's a problem.

It's usually not because I want to be lazy. Most of the time, it's because I'm feeling stressed out and need some sort of escape. This is especially true when the kids are being clingy or difficult and I can't get real, quality "me time". The portable escape of a game on my phone fits the bill of being able to do it anytime, anywhere, with just one hand.

Most recently, I discovered a game that's kind of like Pokemon Go but with dinosaurs – where you go around town, collect DNA from the dinosaurs, create dinosaurs, hybridize them, etc. It was fun at first. We would go on family walks and my husband and I would play, help my son play, and we'd bond. My son loves dinosaurs, so it was kind of the perfect game to entice him to go for a walk with us.

However, it definitely became a problem. It was fun, easy to play, and best of all, portable — but that meant that every time I was overwhelmed, it became my go-to escape. When my kids frustrated me, it was all too easy to sit back in a chair and play my game instead of dealing with them or the frustration that they wouldn't listen to me. It gave me an escape when my husband was unable to give me some real alone time.

I kept getting the feeling God wanted me to take a step back from it, but honestly? I'm hard-headed. I didn't want to give it up! Even when I deleted it from my phone, it only lasted a day or two before I re-installed it and kept playing just as before. Plus, I had so many excuses to justify it to myself ("It's just a little fun!" "I need me-time!" "He loves dinosaurs!")

When I started making use of a screen time tracker on my phone, though, I finally realized how much time I was spending on it. I'm kind of mortified to write it here for all to see — but when I looked at the tracking information, it said I was spending an average of an hour and a half a day on pretend dinosaur hunting.

Talk about feeling your heart drop. I looked back guiltily on all the time I spent complaining about not having time to clean or cook or take any time for myself, and yet I was wasting an hour and a half — a good 10% of my waking hours — on a stupid game. I couldn't help but think of all the ways that time could have been better spent!

Heck, with an hour and a half a day, I think I could be decently fluent in another language by now. I could have read countless books! Our house? It could be spotless. Well, maybe not that — but when it comes to other things I could do with my time, there's a plethora of better options.

I've felt Heavenly Father tell me before under other circumstances that time is not a renewable resource. Money? You can always make more. Weight? You can lose weight if you want. Messy house? It can always be cleaned. Those problems can be fixed any time with willpower and a little ingenuity, no question. Some of those problems can even be outsourced to other people.

Time, on the other hand? Try as you might, you cannot make any more of it. Once it's spent, it's gone. No amount of regret, hard work, willpower, wishing on a star, or anything else will ever get it back. So the small window of time you have with your babies, with your toddlers, with your kids, with your husband, with friends, with extended family? That time is so unbelievably precious. It's irreplaceable.

This life goes impossibly fast. Even though in this day and age we are encouraged to do all the things and move faster than ever, it could do you and your family a world of good to slow it down. Try not to rush out the door in the morning. Sit with your family and savor your dinner. Find a way to truly connect with your children before bedtime so they can drift off to sleep with a smile on their face.

Most of all, making the most of every opportunity the Lord has given you is a great way to express gratitude for the time He has provided.

Especially as a law enforcement family, you are well acquainted with the precariousness of life. You know that tomorrow isn't guaranteed. You hear more stories of tragedy than most, too. Stories of people going about their normal, everyday things and dying as a result of someone else's evil or negligence.

You also see all the tragic stories in the news of fallen officers who never get to come home to their families – families who would give anything for just one more day with their beloved spouse and parent. Those stories weigh on you as you empathize with your fellow police wife and imagine what it might feel like if it had been you to get that awful call.

While that would always be a tragedy, by doing everything you can to make every moment as a family count, you can at least help protect yourself against regret. While you can't control what happens out there while your husband is on duty, you can control the decisions you make with your time.

Truly, it's the most valuable commodity God has given you – it's worth using it well.

PRAYER IDEAS

- Express gratitude for the time God has given you on earth and with your family.
- Thank God for the help He can give you in making the right decisions with that time.
- Pray to see areas in your life where you could be making better use of your time.
- Pray for help changing negative time-wasting habits into better ones.

DO MORE OF WHAT MAKES YOU HAPPY

Do not conform to the pattern of this world,
but be transformed by the renewing of your mind.
Then you will be able to test what God's will is:
His good, pleasing and perfect will.
Romans 12:2

Tell me honestly for a second: how much time do you spend doing stuff that makes you, specifically you, happy? As a wife and mom, there's a good chance most of your time is spent "doing" for your husband and your kids. It's understandable, they need a lot from you. Gosh, sometimes the needs seem never-ending, don't they? But even in the midst of that, you have to find time to renew yourself, too, if you want to meet their needs and keep your own sense of mental well-being.

I remember this feeling very well when my son was first born. I felt like I was just a shell of a person – just a thing that provided milk to the baby, rocked it to sleep, and tried to sleep and eat as much as possible. After a few weeks, I realized I didn't even know what I'd do with free time anymore. I literally couldn't think of any interests I had anymore because it seemed like it had been so long since I'd actually done anything for myself.

Maybe it was postpartum hormones, that's absolutely possible, but it's not the only time I've felt like that. I have had other busy times in my life where I've felt like I couldn't make any time for me, and it made me feel deflated. It made me feel like I wasn't even worth spending time on when I had so many other things to do, and that left me feeling dejected.

The thing is, if you're burning the candle at both ends, you're going to burn out really quickly. I'll tell you that with a surety from personal experience. Nonstop "going, going, going" inevitably results in a crash and burn, and that's the last thing you (and your family!) need to happen.

What stops you from doing the things that make you happy? Is it time? Money? Motivation? Energy? Any and all of those things are totally understandable, but they don't negate the fact that you need to make time for you. Sure, there are seasons of life where your "me time" has to be considerably shorter and simpler, but I promise – it never needs to go away completely. You just have to prioritize.

I know that can be easier said than done. Even if it's just for a few minutes a day, you need to do the things that feed your soul. Do you like painting? Reading? Writing? Sketching? Yoga? Whatever it is, carve out a little time to make it happen. Even 5-10 minutes a day can make a huge difference in your mood.

Start by checking your day for those little time wasters that do nothing to feed your soul. Could you cut out 15 minutes of scrolling through Instagram? Maybe turn off the TV? Unless TV is your "me time", then maybe you could sneak in a few minutes while folding the laundry or prop your phone up on the sink and stream a video while you do dishes.

It might feel selfish to take that time at first, especially when you have kids. Mom guilt is so real. And sure, your life is busy and overwhelming. I don't know if there's anybody who doesn't feel like their life is too busy and overwhelming to do certain things. While you can't do everything, you can definitely carve out time for the things that matter most to you.

The other important aspect of pursuing your passions is that seeing Mom be engaged in something she loves can inspire your kids to find their passions, too.. After all, isn't that what we want for our kids? To be happy and satisfied with their lives, rather than just going through the motions and doing things that don't light up their souls? If you want them to have a happy, fulfilled life, you have to model it for them or they won't know how.

You can also inspire your husband to find "me time", too. Yes, he does a lot with law enforcement, but with work, home, parenting, marriage — all the things, he gets burned out too. You can encourage him to follow his passions, as well — or even find something you guys can be passionate about together! No matter what it is, when you see what a difference it makes for you to have your personal time, you'll want him to reap the benefits, too.

There's no doubt about it: using your time to pursue the things that make you happiest benefits you and everyone else around you.

The flipside of pursuing your passions is to recognize when you're overdoing it. Learn to see when you're overwhelmed and need to step back a little bit. You have to learn to be your own advocate, something that is hopefully easier after boosting your own self-confidence in the last section.

Part of seeking out your happiness is reducing the activities in your life that make you unhappy. I mean, sure there's always going to be things you have to do even though you don't like them. It's important to your mental health to reduce those things as much as possible. When it's not possible, a change in mindset (or method) might be in order.

For instance, let's talk about doing the dishes. Boring, annoying – I get it. We don't have a dishwasher, and it can be a pain. They have to be done, though, so what can you do to enjoy them? For me, dishes have become my time to guilt-freely watch whatever I want to watch on Netflix, since I'm being productive. If I'm in a particularly trying phase and something needs to give, I guilt-freely buy a pack of paper plates and bowls to give myself a break.

Even if pursuing your passions requires you to involve your kids, it's still beneficial! For instance, if you love painting, let the kids paint, too. Watercolors are great and easy to clean up if you're wanting to avoid a giant mess, and they provide a way for your kids to hang out with Mom. If you love hiking, find some kid-friendly trails and make it happen. Want to read a book? Read it out loud while your kids are playing (you know, abridging as necessary).

Whatever you need to do to make yourself happy, take the time to do it. Feed your soul, and you'll not only benefit, but your whole family will as well because they'll have a happier mom and wife. You set the tone for your whole household, so do what you can to make it a good one.

PRAYER IDEAS

- Express gratitude to God for giving you the passions you have.
- Thank God for helping you figure out how to be happier.
- Pray for help making time for the things that make you happy.
- If you're not sure where to start, pray for help determining what you need to make more time for.
- Pray for help in discerning what you need to let go of to make more time for the things that matter most.

REFUGE

47

TRUST HIM WITH EVERYTHING

If that is how God clothes the grass of the field, which is here today and tomorrow is thrown into the fire, will he not much more clothe you?
Matthew 6:30

I've always been fiercely independent. I never wanted to have to depend on anyone else to make things happen for me. As such, I would make my own plans. I would pave my own way. I didn't want to let anyone else be in charge of the things that were most important to me, because I didn't trust that they could take care of them. I didn't trust that they could take care of me.

I extensively studied and planned for everything I needed or wanted to do. I was always taking the bull by the horns to make sure I got the things I wanted and needed most, because if I failed, I at least knew it was all on me. I didn't have anyone else to blame, for better or worse.

This is one of the top things God has been working to fix in me over the past few years, because being fiercely independent like this isn't all that compatible with the humility necessary to follow God's plan for me. As such, every plan I've made over the past few years has crashed and burned if I didn't seek His advice first. The more detailed and extensively I planned by myself, the more off-road my journey seemed to go.

While it's been frustrating at times, the more I've realized what He was trying to do and accepted His will for me and my family, the more at peace I've felt. That has been even more true during the most severe trials. That's not to say it has always been easy – just that through leaning into Him, I have been able to go through those trials without hurting so badly.

The scripture at the beginning of this chapter is so special to me. It's one I associate with one of the strongest spiritual experiences I've had – top 5 for sure. There was a day I was trying to play outside with my son, but was so stressed out I could barely even focus. I sat on my front step trying to take a deep breath and relax, when I looked out at the lawn and thought of this scripture. When I did, I felt completely at peace. The grass and flowers were so beautiful, and having faith in this felt so soothing. I knew in that moment it was so completely true.

This also goes along with the necessity of being like a little child to enter the kingdom of heaven. When I think about it, my son doesn't worry about what he'll eat or what he'll wear. He just goes to the kitchen and gets a snack, or asks me to prepare a meal for him and knows I'll take care of it. He doesn't worry about what he'll wear, because he knows his loving mom has filled his dresser with dinosaur shirts he loves to wear. He knows without question that he will be provided for and doesn't have to worry about whether Mommy will come through or not. It's a given.

Likewise, and even moreso, God is there for us. He isn't going to let us down. If we put our trust in Him, it will never be misplaced. It's never going to backfire on us and ruin things. Things may not work out as we expected, and sometimes they will look like they have indeed failed, but He has promised they will work out for the best. That He will make them work out for the best. After all, He sees the complete puzzle – not just the bits and pieces we're trying so desperately to jam together.

Trusting in God's ability to provide for you and your family takes a lot of stress off your overfilled plate. You can trust Him because He has already promised to take care of everything you need. After all, if you believe God can heal the sick, give sight to the blind, help the lame walk, give the deaf the ability to hear, why couldn't he rescue you from your infirmities, too? He loves you more than you can imagine, and can (and will!) use His power for your good.

As Matthew 6:34 says, "Do not worry about tomorrow, for tomorrow will worry about itself; each day has enough trouble of its own." Seriously, all you need to do is pray about what God needs you to do next and He can and will take care of the rest – just as long as you do what you can to follow what He has asked you to do in the meantime.

Not sure what to do next? Take a deep breath, say a quick prayer, then triage. What's your next best step – the thing that will make everything else a little easier? Maybe it's letting the baby cry while you get a snack for your older kids so they're settled while you care for the baby. Maybe it's cleaning your entry way so you at least feel calm when you first walk in the house. Maybe it's taking a nap when your kids do so you have more energy to parent when they wake up.

Whatever your next best thing is that's in your power, make it happen. If there are things in your control to do, don't hesitate to do them. If you're not sure what to do, pray and ask for help, and know that He will give you the answers you need.

But as for the things that are out of your control? Let them go. Don't worry about what's to come because, as Matthew states, each day has enough trouble of its own. Sometimes it seems like each hour has enough trouble of its own, to be honest — so if you need to take things hour by hour, feel free to do that, too!

Above everything else, trust that God has got your back and will help you in every struggle you face. Do what you can, then take a deep breath, and allow Him to work everything out - as He always has, and forever will.

PRAYER IDEAS

- Express gratitude for God's promise to make all things work together for your good (see: Romans 8:28)
- Thank Him for taking such good care of you.
- Pray for help trusting Him more.
- Pray for assurance that He will take care of the things you're afraid of.
- Pray specifically for help with the things you fear most.

PEACEFUL MARRIAGE

Then the Lord God made a woman from the rib he had taken out of the man,
and he brought her to the man. The man said, "This is now bone of my bones
and flesh of my flesh; she shall be called 'woman,' for she was taken out of man."
That is why a man leaves his father and mother and is united to his wife,
and they become one flesh.
Genesis 2:22-24

If there's one thing I enjoy much more after being married, it's going to weddings. I've always enjoyed them, don't get me wrong, but they are significantly better now that I've experienced one of my own. I've experienced the same thing with babies, actually, but that's beside the point.

There's something so sweet about watching that kind of commitment being made. You're seeing the start of something new, and with that "newness" comes the requisite excitement from everyone around. From the bride, the groom, the families, the friends – everyone. There's a certain "buzz" in the air that just can't be beat. I love everything about it. The inevitable cake is obviously the cherry on top of it all.

But honestly, seeing all those things brings me back to my own wedding. I remember how exciting everything was, how in love we were. The anticipation, the feeling that "Finally, it's here!" How we thought we could never love each other more than we did in that moment. There was fear, of course – going into that kind of commitment is always going to be scary. But we were in love, confident, and completely high on life.

At the same time, in reflecting on our years of marriage, I realize that that day was only the beginning. At the time, it felt like the culmination of our relationship, the "we got married and lived happily ever after" moment, but now, of course, we know better. The truth isn't quite that simple, or quite that blissful – but it's also so, so much better.

The thing is, marriage is kind of a weird concept, when you think about it. It brings together two different people, from two different backgrounds, with two separate sets of expectations, two sets of life experiences and things they know and how they perceive the world. Now they have to be a single unit – one flesh – with unified goals and plans.

That means being a team regardless of their separate careers and hobbies, despite parenting disputes, and in the midst of the craziness that life brings with it. Add to that the inherent unpredictability of law enforcement life, and congratulations - you've hit a brand new level of intensity.

Marriage, by definition, is probably one of the hardest things you can ever do successfully. That's true whether one of you is in law enforcement or not. Building a happy marriage that can withstand everything life throws at it takes hard work, every day, for the rest of your life. I can guarantee, though, that it's absolutely worth every difficult moment.

That's the very thing that I can't help but reflect on at every wedding we attend. I look at the glowing newlyweds standing at the altar and want to cry, thinking, "It only gets better from here." Harder, yes – but wonderfully, exquisitely, inexplicably, so much better.

Having someone you can depend on day after day is the greatest gift. Loving someone and knowing they love you back no matter what darkness life brings is the most reassuring thing you can have when you face trials. Knowing that when the whole world is against you, you have someone who's always on your side, even if they're mad or disappointed, is priceless. Having someone who knows your deepest darkest secrets and loves and treasures you anyway, makes all that darkness a whole lot easier to bear.

When you're a married to a man in law enforcement, the darkness of the world undoubtedly takes on new shades. You hear the worst of the worst, and that's just from what he tells you. I guarantee that for every miserably awful story your husband has told you, he probably has one he doesn't ever want to tell you about. Not because he doesn't love, trust, or respect you — but simply because it's that upsetting. That's bound to have an impact on both of you, no matter how tough you are.

However, that's what makes your marriage that much more important. It's the reason you both have to fight that much harder to make things work. It's that very struggle that makes what you and your husband have that much more powerful — for the two of you, for your family, and even for the world.

Of course, it can be hard to feel completely secure sometimes in the idea of a stable marriage for a lifetime, especially when you see such bleak marriage statistics, particularly for law enforcement marriages. Try not to dwell on those, but to take them as a much-needed reminder to prioritize your marriage and reconnect regularly so nothing drives a wedge between you and your love.

Having a strong, stable marriage doesn't just benefit you and your husband. It benefits everybody else, too — especially your kids. It teaches them what a respectful, healthy relationship looks like. It makes them feel more secure knowing that Mommy and Daddy aren't going anywhere. They don't have to be afraid of their family disintegrating, because its founders, so to speak, are solid.

Statistics back this idea up, too. A 2010 study by the Centers for Disease Control showed children growing up in a home with two married parents did better in every category than children growing up with unmarried or separated parents – in physical and emotional health, in behavior, in GPA; in literally everything. A solid marriage benefits your kids in every single area of their lives, no matter how old-fashioned people may claim it is. Those statistics don't lie.

Improving your marriage benefits others around you, too. You can be a source of strength for others who are struggling, because they know they have both of you to depend on. You can unite with your spouse to help others in their times of need, because each of you has different strengths to draw on. You're a stronger force for good together than either of you could be on your own.

Also, through building up your own marriage, you can inspire others to do the same. When you have been through the fire with your spouse and come out better for it, you can encourage others to keep fighting through their trials, too, letting them know from experience that it's worth it.

In short, it's important to realize that no matter what it takes to have a happy, strong marriage, it is absolutely, 100% worth the effort. You and your husband will always be stronger together. If you want to change the world, start by changing your marriage into the marriage of your dreams - your true happily ever after.

This chapter is all about making that happen by making sure your marriage is as peaceful as possible.

SECTIONS

- Choosing Your Spouse Every Day
- Bear One Another's Burdens
- Making Each Day Count
- A Good Marriage Is Made of Good Forgivers
- You're Designed For Each Other

CHOOSING YOUR SPOUSE EVERY DAY

So they are no longer two, but one flesh.
Therefore what God has joined together, let no one separate.
Matthew 19:6

I've lost my wedding rings way too many times in the years I've been married to my husband, and it's taken me a ridiculous amount of time to find them again. For instance, I misplaced them when I was about eight weeks pregnant with my daughter and didn't find them again until nine weeks after she was born. No joke.

Weirdly enough, the same thing happened when I was pregnant with my son. I'm not sure what the deal is there. Maybe pregnancy brain?

In any case, I was so grateful to my husband when he found them. I remember I was lying in the grass outside, listening to an audiobook and snuggling our baby girl. He came outside to check on us and take a break from cleaning out our bedroom closet. As he headed back inside, I reminded him to keep an eye out for my rings. He got this quirky smile and said, "Look under your pillow."

I was so excited, I could barely contain myself. I jumped up from where I was lying and said, "Bring them out!" because I didn't think I could wait long enough to actually go inside. He met me in the stairway to our apartment and gave them to me. When he did, I couldn't help but think it felt a little like a proposal – and that really got me thinking the next few days as I reminisced on all the history we had together.

We haven't always had the perfect relationship. From the outside, friends would always say, "You guys are so perfect together." In reality, we weren't. We love each other fiercely, but *perfect* for each other? We've both frustrated each other a lot over the years. I mean, I look back on the person I was when I first met my husband and cringe. I can't believe he loved me through that. I'm so thankful he had the patience and wisdom to see who I could really be, and trusting God that I could get there.

Thinking about our history together got me thinking about all the times we've had to choose each other. Every time we've had to say yes to each other, even when it was hard. I think about times of broken hearts, broken promises, and broken trust, and how each time we've chosen each other anyway. I think about every hard time when walking away might have seemed easier, and we chose each other anyway.

Is it because we're perfect — together or as individuals? No, absolutely not. Rather, it's because we knew it would be better to make it work together versus being anywhere else, alone or with anyone else. We know we make a good team, and it wouldn't be worth sacrificing for anything.

What does it really mean to choose each other, though? Choosing your spouse is about choosing the things that will make both of you happy, even when you want to just choose what will make you most happy. It's about choosing to respect each other even when (possibly especially when) you disagree with one another.

It's not about becoming a martyr to the cause. Sacrifice is necessary to making your marriage work, but it shouldn't be one-sided for the long-term. It's not about being a doormat, after all. It is about being willing to settle here and there, and when the inevitable seasons of live come when it's unequal, being able to sustain yourself on the good times.

It's about being a safe harbor to one another — to loving and supporting one another, even when things are hard. Even when you're upset with each other for one reason or another. It means you still kiss, hug, and hold hands as soon as possible, even when you might be furious with each other.

It's about being intentional about your relationship and being as present as possible in a world of never-ending distractions. That means making sure you put each other first over other less important pursuits, like video games or other hobbies. That's not to say those things can never play a role in your life, just that they need to be used mindfully.

Choosing each other means actively living your love for each other in big ways and small. It means doing something a little extra to make each other's day. It means letting the other person be right sometimes (even when you just know you're right and they're wrong). It means being willing to be the first to apologize, even if you feel like they have more to apologize for.

It means being respectful to each other, both when speaking to each other and behind each other's backs. Words are powerful, and knowing love and respect go hand-in-hand means you're careful not to disparage your spouse to others, even if you think they won't find out what you've said

Actively living this kind of love and having a spouse who tries to do the same is a huge step in having a home that is truly a refuge from the storms of life.

With that being said, how can you choose each other every single time?

First, remember that you *will* be tried and tested throughout your marriage No ifs, ands, or buts about it, it's going to happen. Both good things and bad things will ignite change, and change means turbulence. A new baby, a new job, a new shift, a new health crisis, whatever – all these things mean reconfiguring how you did things before and figuring each other out again to determine your new "normal".

Knowing that the changes are coming ahead of time can help you get through it. You can prepare ahead of time, take a deep breath, and move forward anyway, knowing that you will get through this season. That it really is only a season, and that once it passes, you'll both be better – as individuals and as a couple.

As you slowly knit your lives together, your love becomes deeper. It becomes better. It becomes easier and more wonderful – to the point that rather than wistfully looking back on the excitement of being a newlywed, you'll think about yourselves back then with almost a sense of pity. You'll realize that as happy as you thought you were that day, you could never have foreseen the happiness you have now. You'll look back and think about how much better you've both become. You will end up being thankful for everything that has gotten you to that point.

Second, know why you're choosing each other. When tempers flare, when mistakes are made, when feelings get hurt, you have to, in your heart, be able to remember the reasons your marriage is so important. Those are the times that knowing what makes your spouse worth fighting for have to override the current emotional hurt.

Sometimes it takes a lot of mental fortitude to choose your spouse. My husband and I have both made mistakes in the past that hurt each other. Sometimes those were small, everyday mistakes like snapping at each other or missing an emotional cue inadvertently. Some were much bigger ones that we had to work over time to make right with each other.

In those moments, choosing your spouse is not easy. In those moments, loving your spouse is much, much more than just a feeling. It's about knowing who they really are, and knowing that they're more than their mistakes. It's about magnifying their good qualities and letting their bad ones slide, as much as possible. In the end, it's a choice you have to make: to focus on the good, even when you are faced with the bad.

Third, don't be afraid to get help when you need it. There's no shame in marriage counseling and, in fact, many departments actually offer it to officers for free because it's so common to need help in that area. Seeing a marriage counselor doesn't mean there's anything wrong with you or your husband – it just means you need a little outside help to get on the same page. That's okay!

When it comes down to it, sometimes love feels more like a choice than other times. Sometimes it will come easily and things will flow effortlessly. Sometimes the warm fuzzy feelings will come after tears, after struggle, and after a lot of soul-searching. But when it comes right down to it, loving your spouse is always a choice – and it's the best choice you can make, every single day.

PRAYER IDEAS

- Express gratitude for the husband God has provided you.
- Pray for the eyes to see the good in your husband, even (especially!) in the moments that are hard.
- Pray for a softened heart toward your husband when you're feeling frustrated by him.
- Pray for your husband to see your effort – and to see his effort more clearly.
- Pray for help showing your husband grace when you're frustrated with him – and vice versa.
- Ask for the eyes to see the ways in which you've chosen other things above your spouse, and help fixing them.

BEAR ONE ANOTHER'S BURDENS

Carry each other's burdens, and in this way you will fulfill the law of Christ.
Galatians 6:2

I've noticed that my husband and I have the tendency to alternate who is the calm one and who is the stressed out one. Sometimes I'll freak out over the state of the house, and he's super calm, telling me it will all be okay and to get some sleep before I get back to worrying about it. Other times, he'll be completely stressed about an unexpected expense, and I'm cool as a cucumber, telling him it's not such a big deal.

We rarely ever find ourselves freaking out about things at the same time. While it's obviously better when we're both calm at the same time, it's a wonderful gift to know we have the other to buoy us up when we start to sink. It's a blessing to be able to balance each other that way.

I don't think it's just chance, though. I think it's more about the fact that when we see the other one in pain, our first instinct isn't to share in it, but to lift and rescue. We want to relieve the anxiety from each other as best we can — which is part of what it means to bear one another's burdens.

The fact is, life gets tough. Just when you feel like you've gotten a handle on things, your husband will switch from night shift to swing shift and throw everything out of whack. Or your child who has previously had no issues sleeping through the night is up throughout the night for whatever reason, asking you to talk dinosaurs when all you want to do is get precious sleep. Or a sickness makes its way through your household for a solid month.

That's really just scratching the surface with the things that affect you jointly. Personal issues also come up that can make you both struggle. He might deal with a call on shift that leaves him full of questions and regret (even if he did everything right!) and you're tasked with trying to help talk him off the figurative ledge. You might struggle emotionally with an issue with your own workplace, and need him to give you new perspective. Life is full of trials that can bring you down.

Nobody escapes life unscathed, and sometimes things just stink. Whatever those things are, they're significantly less awful when you have help. Personally, I know that the hardest times I've ever had in my life were when I felt like I had to bear my burdens on my own. The more people I am able to reach out to and depend on for help or even just a listening ear, the less I feel the impact of that pain.

Most importantly, though, being able to connect with my husband when I'm in the depths of sorrow is the most important thing. He's the one person in my life who knows me best, which means he knows how best to calm me down. He knows the ins and outs of what I'm struggling with, which means he can give me the best advice.

It hasn't always been that way. Truthfully, we've both had to experience some trial and errors over the year to figure each other out better. That's normal, though, and completely okay. It's part of the marriage process, when it comes down to it, so if you're not there yet, don't feel discouraged. You learn and grow throughout your lifetime, both together and separately.

Being there for your husband in hard times means focusing on what they need from you, rather than assuming you know what's best for them and overpowering their will with yours. Sometimes it's simply in the magic of knowing your spouse well enough to identify when they're struggling even when nobody else can – which, again, can take some time to figure out.

Being there for each other doesn't have to be through huge gestures or epic cryfests. After all, you're married to a law enforcement officer. They're not always big on expressing their emotions or even telling you stories from their day. That's okay. Being there for your husband can be as simple as saying, "It seems like you're feeling stressed out. How can I help?" or allowing them to veg out with video games occasionally without pressure to interact or recap their day with you.

Heck, sometimes just a gentle squeeze of his hand can let him know you're there for him, even if he isn't ready to talk about what's eating at him – which can happen a lot after something traumatic happens on shift. He may not want to talk to you about the specifics. He may even seem mad at you when what he's really feeling is fear, heartbreak, or even regret. No matter the case, knowing you will always be there to love him through everything is incredibly soothing to a troubled heart.

Most importantly, remember that being there by his side emotionally is more important than finding solutions or silver linings. He may not want you to help him figure things out, but just to listen. You don't have to rush him to grieve whatever he's struggling with or make things good again as soon as possible. More than solutions, people generally just want to feel acknowledged. You can remind him it's okay to not be okay – that you'll be there for him through everything.

God's only hands on the earth are yours and mine, which means we have to be there. We have to show up. We have to show the people we love that we are always there for them and that they're not alone in what they're faced with. The person who you can be there for most, the person who needs you most, is the one who you've chosen as your partner in this life.

Being there for each other is so powerful. It means you know you'll never have to carry your burdens alone – that you'll always have a loving, invested helping hand. It makes every weight you have to carry so much lighter. Knowing that you don't have to do it all by yourself makes your marriage that much more important and that much more wonderful.

PRAYER IDEAS

- Express gratitude for the gift of having a partner who can share your burdens, making them easier to carry.
- Thank God for providing you the husband you have, imperfections and all.
- Pray for help knowing what your husband needs most, especially when he takes his frustrations/sadness out on you.
- Pray to understand your husband's problems better, especially when he's having trouble communicating them himself.
- Pray to know how to express your problems to your husband

so he can support you as best he can.

MAKING EACH DAY COUNT

Therefore do not worry about tomorrow, for tomorrow will worry about itself.
Each day has enough trouble of its own.
Matthew 6:34

You know the feeling. You're scrolling through Facebook, and there it is: a news report of another line-of-duty death. Your heart constricts, and all the thoughts run through your mind. All the "what-ifs": What if it had been him? What if it starts riots? What if he gets targeted? What would happen to us?

Then you check the comments (even though you know you never should) and it's all downhill from there. Seriously, don't ever read the comments.

When an officer is harmed, no matter how close or far from home, it brings to light all the anxieties you try to keep so carefully tucked away in your mind. It makes them feel real. It makes them feel so much more likely to happen. When you realize another police wife is now facing the hard reality of being without her officer, it is absolutely terrifying.

The truth is, those days are one of the hardest parts about being married to a man in law enforcement. When you have to send him to work after hearing of a fallen brother in blue, it's natural for your mind to start racing. Logically, another officer's injury doesn't actually mean your husband is more likely to be hurt on shift. He is always in danger. You know that, of course, but emotionally, every news report, Facebook post, or text message brings those dangers to the forefront of your mind.

When you're faced with those thoughts, sometimes you start wondering what would happen if today was the last day you had with your husband. Did you send him off with a hug, a kiss, and an "I love you"? Or was it a hasty wave while you negotiated with your kids about something ridiculous? Or did you barely acknowledge he'd left the house because you were mad at him for breaking his promise to put his dirty clothes in the hamper? Was the last day you had with him the perfect day, one you would treasure forever, or one that would make you feel full of regret?

The biggest anxiety-inducing part of being married to an officer is the reminder of how fragile life is for all of us. It's the fact that you worry every day that it could be the last, that this time, you'll be the wife who receives the news that shatters your heart forever. That fear is unfortunately never going away. On the other hand, the reminder of how tenuous life is can be a blessing if you use it the right way.

After all, life has always been scary. Life is inherently unpredictable and risky. There are smokers that live to be 100 and 17-year-old kids who die from a silent heart condition. It's not morbid or bleak, it's just a fact: nobody gets out of here alive, after all.

That isn't to say it's pleasant to have the fragility of life rubbed in your face as a police wife. At the same time, though, it means that unpredictability is not a secret. It's no surprise to you. Being fully aware of the uncertainty of life can be a constant reminder of why you should be afraid — but on the other hand, it can be your daily reminder to do just a little better.

There's something to be said for the change in perspective that knowledge can bring. Knowing how precarious life can be can help you treat the time you have more reverently. If you let it, the knowledge that life is short can help you be more grateful for the man you married and the life you lead together. It can smooth over disappointments and bring into focus the things that matter most. Maybe most importantly, it can help you forgive your spouse a little more quickly rather than focusing how they've fallen short.

Rather than worry about whether this day could be "the day", focus on what you can control: making your days with him count. Let that fear of the worst possible outcome fuel your desire to forgive quickly, celebrate the good about him, and always kiss good-bye before he starts his shifts — even if he's done something that has made you absolutely livid at him. It's not worth holding that grudge, if the worst were to happen.

As a police wife, you have a really special opportunity to understand the secret that having a happy marriage isn't about the occasional big special things you do for each other. A happy marriage is built on the little things, the small acts of kindness, you do for one another every single day, because all the time you have together counts.

Let's be clear, though. I'm not saying you're going to read this chapter and never have a fight again. Don't feel guilty for the days you come up short. Even if that day were to become "the day", I don't want you to feel like you have failed, because you haven't. Instead, keep it simple: aim for a nice 5:1 ratio of good moments to bad ones with your husband.

That means for every negative moment you have with your husband, try to intentionally facilitate five good ones. They really don't have to be big. A hug can count as one of those good interactions.

The key, though, is being aware of having an overwhelmingly positive relationship with your husband, most of the time, so the good stuff comes more regularly.

If you need some more ideas for little positive interactions with your husband, here's a short list:

- Say a prayer with/for him.
- Kiss him before he heads out the door.
- Say I love you.
- Leave a note in his lunch box or on the bathroom mirror.
- Ask about his day and really listen to his answer.
- Text him something nice during the day.
- Say "thank you" for something you noticed he did around the house.

The point is, when you go out of your way to make the everyday mundane things of life as special as possible, you don't have to live in regret if something were to happen – to either one of you! Let that thought give you freedom from the anxiety of police wife life, and redirect that energy to what you actually have control over.

Treat your husband lovingly as often as possible, making the best choices you can, and you will never have to live in regret, no matter what happens.

PRAYER IDEAS

- Express gratitude for the time God has given you with your husband.
- Thank God for keeping you both safe so that you can continue to love and support one another on the earth.
- Pray to know what to do today to improve your relationship
with your husband.
- Pray for help knowing how to make today the best day you can for both you and your husband.
- Ask how you can best serve your husband today – what does
he need most from you?
- Ask for help making sure your needs are met by your husband
– that you can communicate them effectively and that he will understand you.

A GOOD MARRIAGE IS MADE OF GOOD FORGIVERS

Bear with each other and forgive one another
if any of you has a grievance against someone.
Forgive as the Lord forgave you.
Colossians 3:13

I've always been touched by stories of people forgiving severe wrongdoings. The stories of people who have lost a brother, a sister, a mother – or even a whole family – to the carelessness of other people, or even straight-up evil, and yet forgive those people for it? They dumbfound me.

After all, I've never been a natural forgiver. I've always been more inclined to grudge-holding and vengeance-seeking. I want things to be fair, and it feels so wrong when they can't be. My natural tendency is toward eye-for-eye justice, not grace. But as with my other faults, I've witnessed Heavenly Father work to break down that tendency over time.

I've had my fair share of hurts over the past few years – some big, some small. But in every case, I've had to learn how to forgive. Honestly, though, I think the most important thing I've learned over the years is *why* I should forgive. I've learned how forgiveness frees *me*, not the person who has done me wrong. I've learned how forgiveness heals me – and can heal the person who has done me wrong, if they want redemption. I've learned that people who hurt others are usually hurting themselves, and Heavenly Father has softened my heart enough to feel heartbroken for them, too.

True happiness comes from being able to forgive and forget as quickly as possible — and there's no better place that comes into play more than your marriage. Honestly, sometimes it almost seems easier to forgive acquaintances for hurting you because you don't have to see them every day. You don't necessarily have to work things out with them. You can just each go your own way, no hard feelings, and move on from the experience.

On the other hand, when it comes to your spouse, it's easy to let perceived wrongdoings build up between you. He's been working too much. He's on a lousy shift that means you usually just see him sleeping. He's been short with the kids for one reason or another. The house is a mess and you're mad because he didn't clean something you asked him to take care of. He comes home in a grouchy mood and snaps at you for the one thing you didn't do, even though you've worked your butt off all day.

It happens to everyone, and, trust me, I know how frustrating it gets. The resentment can build and eventually, I explode — either at him, at the kids, or just have a soda-and-chocolate fueled self-destructive meltdown. When I focus on what I need and how unfair things feel on my end, I can't help but lose my cool a little, one way or another.

Plus, all that resentment just breeds more resentment. Past hurts make me assume the worst about my husband, which means that's what I'm looking for. If he gets home and I assume he's going to frustrate me, there's a good chance I'll be looking for reasons to be frustrated by him. What you look for is what you'll find, and looking for the worst pretty much ensures we'll have a lousy evening together.

Instead of holding on to those past hurts, what would happen if you allowed your husband the freedom of a clean slate, every morning – just like Heavenly Father offers you? Forget about everything your spouse has done up until now to give you grief. Let each other have a clean slate, and see how it changes things.

That's not to say you should just sweep everything under the rug. That's not what forgiveness is about. It's okay (and good, and totally healthy!) to tell you husband what's eating at you. Just do so diplomatically – "I" statements and all that. There's no need to attack him for doing something wrong, any more than you'd want him to lambast you for your mistakes.

Where the forgiveness part comes in here is deciding to air your grievance or straight up let it go – and then, either way, let it go. For good. For real. It's letting it go completely, not tucking it away in your back pocket for use during an argument. That's not fair. Instead, literally, once it's dealt with, don't bring it up again. Move forward, and don't think about them again.

Honestly, what can be hardest for me is deciding what to mention and what to straight up let go of. I usually err on the side of "not wanting to ruin my husband's day" rather than discussing what's bothering me, and it makes for a lot of less-than-resolved problems if I let that tendency take over.

Like pretty much everything else I'm unsure about, that's where prayer comes in. I ask for help forgiving him and not being grumpy, and ask whether I need to discuss it or not. If I do it that way, I'm usually able to bring things to light the right way (read: diplomatically, not freaking out) and we can move along with the rest of our day a lot easier.

Even if it starts a fight, that's okay. It's all communication in the end. The best thing about marriage is that even if the fights sometimes hurt you or the other person, you have all sorts of time to heal. You have love, a rapport, and a feeling of confidence in one another that can help you through, as long as you bring things to light in the right way.

God can also help you see one another through fresh eyes. When you're completely at your wit's end with your husband (or vice versa), praying to see your spouse as God sees them is extremely helpful. It allows you see things from a new perspective and give you the right words to say in every tricky situation. God is incredibly invested in your relationship, and He isn't going to let you down.

He can help you not only have the confidence to confront difficult situations, but also give you the right words to say at the right time to get your point across. He can help your words be received gracefully and in the spirit you mean them in, and help you better understand your husband's response in the way he meant it, too. He knows you both perfectly and can help bridge the gaps between you.

While frustrating situations still come up, adopting this attitude helps me see my husband through eyes of grace. It helps me be more gentle and forgiving. It also helps me communicate better, because I can explain what's frustrating me in the moment rather than having a deluge of past frustrations I'm trying to punish him for.

Another trick you can use if you're struggling to offer your husband a clean slate each day is going back to the beginning of your marriage. Think about your wedding day. Bring back all that hope and lovey-dovey-ness. What would that look like? Would you hold grudges, or would you forgive more quickly? Would you be quick to do nice things for him, regardless of what you've been through during the day?

Forgiveness isn't always easy. But God can always help you when you're struggling to forgive, especially when it comes to your husband.

He is the only one who can take your pain, soothe it, and help it feel like you don't have to carry anything at all.

Forgiveness is the power that allows us to bear heavy burdens lightly, so keep practicing forgiveness as often as possible. You will both be all the happier for it.

PRAYER IDEAS

- Express gratitude for the opportunity to grow more like Him and more in love with your husband through the power of forgiveness.
- Thank God for forgiving you for your sins, allowing you to start fresh each day.
- Ask for help starting fresh with your husband today, no matter what happened yesterday.
- Ask for help letting the painful things of the past go and becoming better, not worse, as a result of them.
- Ask to see the hurt behind every hurtful decision your husband makes.
- Ask if there is any action you've taken that has come between you and your husband, and ask how to make it right.

YOU'RE DESIGNED FOR EACH OTHER

Above all, love each other deeply, because love covers over a multitude of sins.
1 Peter 4:8

My husband is well-known for his impeccable sense of people. It's amazing and incredibly frustrating, all at the same time. We'll meet someone at, say, a party, for instance. I'll think they're great, but he'll say something like, "I don't know, there's just something off about them." I'll try to refute it, but inevitably, he will end up being right. Maybe not right away, but eventually, somehow, he is always right.

Honestly, it's my favorite and least favorite thing about him, all in one. I like it because I trust his feeling about people implicitly, and I know he can help keep me and our kids safe. It's also a smidge disheartening because I know where that talent comes from: experience.

The thing is, he is all too familiar with the evils of the world. He's seen it firsthand, both in personal dealings with people and in law enforcement. He's dealt with it. He has seen things I can scarcely imagine, worked with people who I think would make me pee my pants if I met them in real life. Plus, he had to take care of them so they didn't hurt themselves or anyone else. That's enough to make anyone a little jaded.

It's not that I believe everyone is good and the world is bright and shiny. It's more that I would really, really like to believe those things. I want to think everyone has good intentions, even if they screw up occasionally. I'm admittedly kind of a softie. I tend toward trying to find an excuse for other people's shortcomings, even if the excuses are a reach.

It may not surprise you that this tendency sometimes annoys my husband. He accuses me of being too naïve, like the time I nearly got hustled by one of the "street monks" when we were on vacation in Las Vegas. I sometimes feel like he's being unnecessarily negative, like when he walked right past those monks who "just wanted donations to build a temple". (My bad, babe.)

At times, it's super frustrating for both of us. I don't necessarily love when my belief in humanity has to be trampled on, and he doesn't love to be the one to trample on it, even if it's not really his fault. He also doesn't like being questioned on his judgment when he's seen more of the dark underbelly of humanity than I have. It's fair, really, but frustrating for both of us.

The thing is, this opposition in our personalities, as incompatible as it may seem, actually makes our lives so much better. It isn't even just a matter of naivete or negativity – it's because if we were both married to people who were exactly like us, it wouldn't be pretty.

I mean, can you imagine the disastrous consequences of a couple who always saw people exactly the same way? It would be really hard to make friends as a couple, because potential friends would be prematurely written off for the tiniest reason. On the other hand, a couple where both partners expect the best in people may be more likely to be victims of a scam, or worse, because they didn't anticipate it.

Taking it a step further into the rest of life, opposites are a huge benefit. Part of my optimism is often a "leap first, look later" approach to ideas. If I had a similarly-minded husband, my life would be total chaos. My imaginary doppelganger husband would encourage my every desire to leap, no matter how ill-advised. He'd be enthusiastic, optimistic, and go along with my excitement.

I would start hundreds of projects that would never get a chance to succeed, because I'd get discouraged after a week or two and decide to try something new - without anyone to bring me back to earth and encourage me to stick to it. I'd flit from one thing to another until I was so worn out I couldn't do anything else. I have no doubt I would have a lot more unfinished projects, a lot more debt, and nothing to ground me.

Sure, some of it sounds fun – after all, if I were married to myself, I'd probably convince myself to go on vacation a lot more often than I currently do (hello, Hawaii!) For the most part, though, it sounds pretty exhausting. It sounds like I would do a lot of work for not a lot of payoff.

My husband's life, on the other hand, would be safe to a fault. He and his imaginary doppelganger wife would never take unnecessary risks. Everything would be on hold until they were 100% sure they knew it was the right thing and had a start to finish game plan. Even the smallest decision would be a six-month process of pro/con lists and debates. On some level, it sounds sort of sensible, I guess, but that approach would also translate to way too many missed opportunities.

Where I'm in desperate need of someone to ground me and give me a reality check, my husband needs a jumper, a risk-taker, to get him moving even when he's not totally sure about the direction. Our lack of compatibility in this area, though it can be frustrating for both of us, is actually an amazing benefit of our marriage.

You and your husband probably also have a lot of differences, and many of them probably get under your skin sometimes. Maybe your husband is the money-saver in your relationship and you're more prone to spending. Maybe he's the optimist and you're the pessimist. Maybe he's the planner and you're the "jumper".

Whatever the case may be, I guarantee that in one way or another, you and your husband balance each other. There's a reason "opposites attract" is such a cliché – it's true, and ultimately, beneficial to you in more ways than one.

When you bring different things to the table, you have a better view of every situation. That means you can better assess it. Your kids have different kinds of parents to turn to for different problems. When you need advice, you have someone who loves you, who you trust, who can give you a different spin on what you've already seen.

That's not to say recognizing the benefits will take away all irritation about them. After all, my husband and I still find ourselves getting irritated with our differences. It will, however, give you at least some perspective.

All in all, it's important to think about how you balance each other out and how your differences, even the frustrating ones, make you both better. Because truly, you and your husband were each designed to do just that.

PRAYER IDEAS

- Express gratitude for the differences between yourself and your husband, acknowledging that those things was designed to make each of you better.
- Thank God for the opportunity you and your spouse both have to become better through your marriage.
- Ask for the eyes to see the things that make you so perfectly suited for one another.
- Ask God to help you be less irritated by your husband's differences, and see the positive aspects of them.
- Ask for help seeing things from your husband's perspective, especially when you're frustrated by it.
- Ask for your husband to have the eyes to see your perspective, too – and for help communicating it effectively.

PEACEFUL PARENTING

Start children off on the way they should go,
and even when they are old they will not turn from it.
Proverbs 22:6

It's funny how sometimes the hardest moments in parenting teach you the most. You could say that's the biggest benefit of solo parenting: a plethora of learning opportunities. Because while parenting in and of itself is no walk in the park, when you're doing most of it on your own, it's approximately a thousand times harder.

I had this kind of experience not long ago. I was looking forward to some help over my husband's days off, but he ended up getting a migraine – for two days straight. This meant that, even with him home, I was on my own. Even handing him the baby was out of the question because the sound of her crying made him want to puke.

Talk about extremely un-relaxing time off.

The next day, my husband went back to work, having barely recovered. I said good-bye, then took a deep breath to greet the morning. I needed to try to stave off the feeling of overwhelm that was already beginning to creep in, before the sun had even risen. I managed to keep my cool until it was time to go grocery shopping - you know, that glorious moment of motherhood where you have a specific task to accomplish, and every single obstacle gets in your way.

It's that time when the preschooler will inevitably lose it over you not buying a box of cereal (even though you have a box of that exact one at home.) Then the baby starts crying and you realize she had a blowout, and you have two wipes left – and no backup outfit, so you need to go back and buy a new one. Then the only lane open is self-checkout where everyone is giving you the evil eye because you're taking so darn long.

By the time I got back to the car, I was fully engulfed in overwhelm. I asked my son to go get in his seat while I put the groceries away and put his sister in her seat. I was barely holding on emotionally, and just wanted to get home. That's when my son swung his door open and whacked himself in the head. There was a brief silence, then he started absolutely squalling. I tell you, I could have curled up on the ground right there and cried myself. It was the worst timing ever.

I then had to comfort both kids, because my daughter is very much a sympathy crier, especially when it comes to big brother. My son then cried more, because the baby was crying, and... well, you can see the vicious cycle we were in. When everyone was finally settled, I put them both in the car, took a deep breath, and leaned my head against the steering wheel. Then I thought the only thing I could muster: *God, I need your help.*

When I did so, I immediately, overwhelmingly felt His comfort. More than that, I couldn't help but feel like that precise moment was exactly why He had allowed me to get so overwhelmed. If I hadn't, I might have forgotten to reach out to the ultimate source of comfort. Maybe I would have continued trying to depend on my own strength, my own knowledge. Maybe I would have continued feeling like I was doing things all on my own, forgetting that He was always on my side.

God never gives us trials casually. They are always designed for our benefit, even if we can't necessarily see it past the mounds of toys cluttering up our living rooms. Even if you can't always see it at the time, God sanctifies your most difficult days as a mother. He raises you up and calls you blessed, because you are a vitally important figure in doing His work.

That's because you are the biggest influencer in whether your kids follow God or not, as per the scripture at the beginning of this section. If anyone is going to accomplish shepherding your kids toward salvation, it's more than likely going to be you.

After all, you are part of them. You are the one who helps shape their hearts and minds from the very beginning. When your toddler wanders a few feet away from you, checks where you are, and comes back, you can see that you're her North Star. You're an integral part of their development.

If you're not so sure about that, look at what happens to kids who don't have the benefit of thriving families, whose parents prioritize drugs, sex, alcohol, or anything else over the welfare of their children. Those children struggle without engaged, loving parents. They have more trouble in school. They struggle to relate in healthy ways to their peers. Ultimately, those children often grow up to have the same issues that they witnessed their parents struggle with, because they never saw another way.

It certainly doesn't mean they're doomed forever (on the contrary: God is the ultimate healer!) But it definitely makes it harder to live a happy, fulfilled life as an adult when they have so much of their childhood to heal from. I wouldn't wish that on anyone.

  With how significant your task is, how vital it is to the people your children are destined to become, you can rest assured that God will never leave you to do it all by yourself. He loves you and your children more than you could even imagine, which means He knows what you all need. He knows, He cares, and He has promised never to let you down.

  That being said, it can be hard to rely on this power when you're in the trenches of parenthood. How can you find the rest and comfort you need in God when you can't find a quiet moment all to yourself? When every moment is filled with sibling rivalry, trying to manage the clutter that comes with children, and the huge emotional load of trying to meet all your children's needs, it sometimes feels like survival is the best you can hope for.

  This section is all about learning to parent peacefully by partnering with God in every moment of parenthood – the good, the bad, the hilarious, and the devastating – so you can find confidence in everything you are called to do.

SECTIONS

- They're Yours For A Reason
- Keeping Your Family Safe
- Being Merciful Like He Is
- Lead By Example
- Find Your Tribe

THEY'RE YOURS FOR A REASON

For you created my inmost being;
you knit me together in my mother's womb.
I praise you because I am fearfully and wonderfully made;
your works are wonderful, I know that full well.
Psalm 139:13-14

One of the hardest things I faced when I became a mother was stressing out about whether I was a good enough mom for my son. I distinctly remember being about 36 weeks pregnant and sitting in his nursery, terrified. My husband was at work, so I sat in the new rocking chair, looked at the crib we had put together the day before, and cried. Whether it was the hormones or the realization that he would be coming as soon as the next week, I was terrified, because I was convinced that God had made a mistake in letting me become a mother.

I thought about all the times I had been impatient with kids. I worried about all the things I didn't know yet. I didn't even know how to change a newborn's diaper. And what did I know about breastfeeding? I read all the things, but still felt like I was lacking. I had never been entranced by babies. I've always been a wreck without sleep. I had no idea how I would have the patience, love, and selflessness required to be what my son needed. After all, as I sat there, I had to admit; I was pretty selfish.

I already loved my son so much. I was terrified I would fail him by being too selfish and uninvolved with him. I cried thinking about all the ways I was sure I would fail him. On top of that, I wondered, what if he came and I didn't have that crazy burst of love everyone talks about? I was so terrified of everything motherhood was going to bring that I already felt like I was blowing it — before my baby boy had even come earthside.

After 30 hours of labor (most of which was sans epidural, but who's counting?) and an intense emergency C-section, I discovered how deeply I could actually love. My concerns about not being capable of motherhood turned out to be completely unfounded. I cried when I saw him for the first time, and my first thought upon seeing his little face was, "I love you; I'd do that again if I had to."

Even just after coming out of all that pain and misery, I immediately knew I would do it again if I needed to. I knew I would be willing to do anything for my son, so surely I couldn't completely fail him the way I was worried I might.

I'm not saying I have been the perfect mother from that time forward, but I can say my love for him (and now, for my daughter) has always given me the perspective I needed to make the right decisions for him.

The fact is, you have a maternal instinct for a reason — because you were made to be your children's mother. God has led you through the experiences you've had in your life to mold you into who you need to be for them. He will help you as you go forward and meet you where you are to help you. Your individual strengths and weaknesses are exactly what they need to help them develop.

Over and over again, I've seen this to be true in my own life. I often find myself doing things as a mom that don't necessarily make sense to me (or, you know, those around me). Like homeschooling, for instance. Shortly after my son was born, I felt strongly that I was supposed to, even though I really didn't want to. Over time, though, I've seen my baby boy blossom into a precocious, active, kinetic learner who would absolutely fail in a mainstream school environment. I can see his potential and I know how to nurture it. If I was left to my own devices, without the wisdom given by the Holy Ghost, I might have missed it.

Even in choosing a C-section for my daughter, God has helped me feel confident I can do right by my kids. I struggled for a long time deciding whether to plan a C-section or not, and ultimately, after lots of prayer and a pro/con list or two, I chose to do so. It was such a good thing I did, because she had meconium when she was born. Another day or two in the womb and things might have ended very differently.

Plus, as the surgeon said, I would have ended up on the operating table anyway, so what a relief to be able to plan on it instead.

It can be hard to trust your instincts in this day and age. Everywhere you go – on social media, at the store, on TV –there's mom shame. Whether it's about breastfeeding versus bottle-feeding, cosleeping or sleeping in a crib, or pretty much any other choice you can make as a mom, someone might shame you for it. It adds to the crushing overwhelm of parenting and makes it that much harder to discern the right decisions for your family.

It's especially hard when you end up doing things as a solo parent because your husband is off catching bad guys. It means you might have to settle for allowing more screen time, or more processed meals, or whatever else you need to let slide in favor of survival – things which you may internally battle yourself over because you read the articles about how bad those things are. I know I do the same thing.

In the process of making those decisions, I want to encourage you: you've got this. You don't have to worry about who's judging you or for what. God knows you. He knows you and your kids completely. He fully understands the totality of your situation, which means His is the only opinion you really need to worry about. And best of all, He'll actually give you good advice to make the right decisions when you ask for His help.

He can help you decide what needs to be your priority, and what you can let slide. He can give you promptings about whether you should worry more about screen time, or diet issues, or reading, or whatever else is heavy on your mind. He can help you know when to give yourself a break, or gently encourage you when you need to try a little harder on something.

Remember, God gave you your kids for a reason. Don't forget that you're God's daughter as well and He will take care of you as you take care of them. You are not in this alone, and you never have been. You've got this, and your God is never going to let you down.

PRAYER IDEAS

- Express gratitude for the children God has given you.
- Thank Him for always being there for you, especially in the most challenging moments.
- Ask for the wisdom to see the ways in which you're the right mother for your children.
- Ask for discernment in seeing how your kids have made you a better person.
- Ask for the eyes to see how your challenges with your kids benefit both of you.
- Ask to know what you need to focus on today that will most help your children flourish in the future.

KEEPING YOUR FAMILY SAFE

*But the Advocate, the Holy Spirit, whom the Father will send in my name,
will teach you all things and will remind you of everything I have said to you.*
John 14:26

There are a lot of benefits to being a stay-at-home mom, but I
have to say, the hands-down highlight of my week is my kids' Free
Forest School program. Two or three times a week, I take them out
and meet up with other moms somewhere in the mountains. There,
I get to chat with actual grown-ups and the kids get to play freely in
nature. It's pretty much the best thing ever.

There was one week in the spring where the meeting at our
favorite site was cancelled due to severe wind, the possibility of a
storm later in the day, and because the leader's kids were sick.
However, I didn't know that until about 10 minutes before we were
going to leave. I was bummed out, but figured I had prepared
already, so I might as well just go it alone. After all, if it got too
rainy to stay, we could easily head back home – no harm, no foul.

As I got into the car, however, I got the distinct sense that we
shouldn't go. I groaned internally at the thought of getting the kids
back out of the car. I'd just buckled them in! I knew they would be
happy after going. And frankly, I really wanted to go, too. Especially
because my son had been kind of a pain that morning and I knew
some nature play would reset him. I decided to continue on

anyway, figuring I was just being overly paranoid.

We kept driving, and the closer I got, the stronger the "don't go" feeling became. It got to the point that I could no longer ignore it. Even so, I wasn't completely sure yet whether it was really the Holy Ghost or just my anxiety talking. As such, I decided to "test" it. I turned on music, cleared my mind, got nice and relaxed, then thought about going again.

Boom: it was the same thing. *"Do not go."*

Stubborn as I am, I still wanted to go (I know!), but that last impression was so strong there was no way I could ignore it. Instead of driving to the trail head, I drove right past the turn off and let my son continue playing on his tablet. I took him to a local cafe instead where I got a drink and he got to play with their train table while the baby slept.

I didn't think much on the experience until we met with the group again a few days later. A woman said she and her kids went to that same trailhead the day after we had planned to go. She said her daughter found a severed deer leg, right in the middle of the meadow where we would normally have played.

I was dumbfounded. My guess is that with the weird change in weather, a mountain lion was out hunting. I knew they were up in the area, but had never given them much thought before. I was so grateful I listened to that voice even though it didn't make sense, because God knows and sees more than I do. What would have happened if I had been alone with two kids and faced with a mountain lion? I don't even want to think about it.

Even when we aren't talking about big scary predators like mountain lions, the Holy Ghost can help guide you to keep your family safe. He can let you know when danger is ahead, as long as you do what you can to listen. Even if you're as stubborn as I am, He will make sure to do everything He can to keep you and your family out of danger. I am personally beyond grateful for His persistence!

It can be hard not to feel anxious when you have the burden of information. Thanks to being married to a law enforcement officer, you have a deeper knowledge of the usual suspects, like sex offenders and human traffickers, and even the dangers of people using drugs at local playgrounds. Personally, the thing I'm most scared of when going out with my kids is that they'll step on a needle when we're out and about – and I don't think that would have even been on my radar without my husband.

Fortunately, in much the same way as the mountain lion scenario I described, the Holy Ghost can give you a heads up about the people and situations that could be dangerous for your family. As I have said before, your children are yours for a reason. You're tasked with doing your part to keep them safe, but you're not in it alone. You have help: you just have to pay attention.

Honestly, I think listening to both the Holy Ghost and your instincts can be especially hard for women. Hear me out here: I think we as women tend to want to be more accommodating overall. We don't want to hurt other people's feelings or make a fuss. In all honesty, it's good when we're in a situation that calls for diplomacy. On the other hand, that tendency can sometimes that put us in a perfect position to be hurt.

If the Holy Ghost is telling you to do something, just do it! Even if you're worried it will make you seem rude or even silly. He will never tell you something just to say something. There is always a reason behind the promptings you get. Trust me, I have learned this the hard way at times!

If you find yourself wondering whether the feeling in your gut is real or a product of anxiety (as I sometimes wonder), pray about it. Be explicit - "do you want me to keep the kids home today?" Or, "if you want me to do X, don't let me stop thinking about it. Otherwise, help me forget." And if you're struggling to be obedient, for whatever reason, you can pray about that too!

No matter what, God will give you the knowledge you need to make the right decisions. You just have to listen carefully and ask the right questions. Knowing that, I know that even in the most dangerous places, the Holy Ghost really can empower you to keep your family safe.

PRAYER IDEAS

- Express gratitude for God's promise to watch over you at all times.
- Pray to not be afraid, to walk in peace, as you try to keep your family safe.
- Pray for discernment about the intentions of those around you to know how to keep your kids safe from those with ill will.
- Ask how you can be more receptive to the promptings of the Holy Ghost.
- Ask for help being obedient to those promptings.

BEING MERCIFUL LIKE HE IS

Blessed are the merciful, for they will be shown mercy.
Matthew 5:7

Around our house, I regularly have week-long streaks of my son completely refusing to listen. Sometimes it's because he has a cold coming on, sometimes it's because he's upset with something that happened with a friend, and sometimes it's for no apparent reason. But there was one week that sticks out in my memory because it taught me a significant lesson.

That week, no matter what I said or did, my son would insist on choosing his own way. Inevitably, he would come to regret it, then he would get upset because he made the wrong decision and got hurt, broke something, or both.

It drove me nuts! I kept saying, "Buddy. If you just listened to me, life would be so much easier." I said it so many times, I thought about just recording it on my phone so I could play it on a loop and hopefully I would finally get my point across, plus get a chance to rest my voice a little.

In the middle of one of these tirades, though, I received the Holy Ghost equivalent of a smack upside the head. I had just finished chastising him for not listening for about the thousandth time that day when I heard the Holy Ghost whisper to me, "You don't always listen, either."

Yikes. Talk about being humbled.

Truly – I don't always listen. Sometimes I get the impression that I shouldn't buy that random cute flowerpot from Target, because I'll need that money later. Yet, I don't trust the impression and decide my desire for that random cute flower pot is more important. I later regret it when I realize I've over drafted our bank account, and realize maybe it wasn't so important.

Sometimes I don't bite my tongue when I'm feeling mad, even though I feel like I should, and inevitably want to bury my head in the sand later because I feel so embarrassed of my outburst. Then I have to apologize and make things right, which makes me feel extra embarrassed.

Sometimes I feel like I should stop watching a show or reading a book because it's too dark, and yet I find myself guiltily continuing anyway. Then, of course, I get into a dark mood later because it affected me too much, or I get a lousy night's sleep because I had nightmares, or some combination of the two.

If we're talking about disobedient children, I might just be one of the worst offenders.

Heck, I think about my life prior to finding Christ and cringe. One of the first times I went to church I saw a girl I knew in high school who said, "You got baptized? Wow! That gives me such hope!" Insert embarrassed smile here. I think she meant it as a compliment, but I can't really blame her.

God has had to forgive me for so many things. He has helped me change in so many ways. I find myself feeling so grateful for it, but then sometimes I feel like crying a little when I make yet another mistake (or three, or four – in a day) and realize how much further I have to go.

Fortunately, we have an incredibly merciful Father in Heaven. Do you ever think about all the things God has forgiven you for? All the mistakes you've made, big and small. Every side-eye and mean thing you've ever said, or even thought! He's seen you at your darkest and most humiliating moments and loves you nonetheless – or, just maybe, all the more.

Remembering His mercy should prompt us to find ways to be that much more merciful to those we love – including our children.

What it comes down to is recognizing that the bad behavior of other people, whether it's from your kids, your husband, or anyone else, comes from something they are struggling with. Whether that's feeling sick, sad, scared, jealous, hurt, or whatever. People usually aren't giving you a hard time just to be a jerk. They're doing it because they're hurting.

If you can keep that in mind, it can help you respond with love instead of wrath. Responding mercifully will ensure a much more peaceful home. If you respond to anger and hurt with your own anger and hurt, you end up simply perpetuating the cycle and making things worse.

Responding mercifully to ornery kids, or even an ornery husband, doesn't mean being a doormat to their needs or telling them it's okay to treat you rudely. Being merciful doesn't mean not setting boundaries: it's just about setting them in loving ways. There's nothing bad about telling someone you won't accept a particular way of being treated – but you can connect and improve that relationship by also saying, "Hey, I can see you feel lousy and I love you even though you're being rude. I love you enough to help you through it, but please rephrase."

I'll admit — sometimes it's hard to extend mercy to your kids because it can feel like you're rewarding them for misbehaving, but that's not the case. Your love isn't a reward. Unconditional love is a gift that your kids shouldn't have to earn — because you don't have to earn God's either.

Plus, being loving is way more effective. I'm an adult, and when I'm being rude because I'm having an impossibly hard day, it doesn't make me feel any better if someone is rude back. The moment someone does something nice for me, especially if I don't deserve it, I feel like I want to straighten up and fly right. It means I have the opportunity to face the unpleasant emotion behind my behavior rather than continuing to exhibit the symptom. Kids react in much the same way.

I've experienced this myself, when my son raged during a sick day. He yelled at me, hit me, and kicked me, and I brought him to his room. When I shut the door, I heard him continue to rage. As I listened, I did my best to calm down rather than amp myself up. I prayed, asking God for help on whether I need to punish him further or show him love. The answer was the latter: after time-out, I wrapped him in a big hug. I told him how much I loved him and that I'm always here for him. I then sat down next to him and told him I would not let him hit me and throw things at me. I told him that it's okay to feel sad or mad, even at me, but it wasn't okay to hurt me.

Because I kept my cool and showed him love, the rest of the day went a lot more smoothly than it has in the past. My response built our connection, which built his respect for me. As he gets older and he has bigger decisions to make, he knows he can trust me and my opinion. He can know that even when I'm mad, I'm on his side and can help him navigate life.

That sounds familiar, right? Doesn't that kind of sound like how Heavenly Father deals with us? We must be respectful of Him, but I know I've said angry prayers before. I've asked Him why He would allow me to go through certain things. I've railed against Him because His timing didn't make any sense to me. I've cried about the unfairness of life or because I felt like He didn't care about me because I wasn't seeing the blessings I wanted most.

In each of these circumstances, He spiritually took me into His arms and helped me heal. He gave me comfort. He gave me wisdom to understand why things weren't working like I thought they should. He helped me see the long-term plan, or even just a glimpse of it. He supported me in every moment I was unpleasant either to Him or to those around me, even though I absolutely didn't deserve it. He loves me and sees my heart in every moment of every day, and is willing to address those deeper issues rather than punishing my shortcomings at every turn.

Showing Christlike mercy in the face of difficult situations with your family can truly change everything for the better.

PRAYER IDEAS

- Express gratitude for God's mercy toward you, especially at the times you least deserve it.
- Thank God for knowing your heart; for seeing who you can become, and not just the imperfect person you are today.
- Pray for the eyes to see the hearts of those you love and not just their behavior.
- Pray for more opportunities to develop patience (if you're feeling brave.)
- In the face of difficult behavior from your kids or husband, pray for the wisdom to see the hurt behind it.
- Pray for opportunities to be more merciful with your family.

LEAD BY EXAMPLE

Be shepherds of God's flock that is under your care, watching over them - not because you must, but because you are willing, as God wants you to be; not pursuing dishonest gain but eager to serve; not lording it over those entrusted to you, but leading by example.
1 Peter 5:2-3

I'm constantly struck by how similar my son is to me. For instance, he got a valentine this past February that came with a small sticker-by-number project. When I tried to help him with it, he got mad because he didn't want to follow the instructions. I asked, "Come on, don't you want it to look like the picture?" I was trying to keep my cool, but underneath, I was getting really frustrated.

That's when I had a flashback to when I was about six years old. My siblings and I had all gotten paint by number kits from the store, and I wanted to choose my own colors. I remember my sister getting so frustrated with me and my six-year-old self couldn't understand why. It was *my* painting! Why wouldn't they just let me do it how I wanted?

That's when I realized I was getting mad at my son for being exactly like me.

Honestly, it made me think about all the times I'm a hypocrite as a parent. Like when I complain he's not listening and he should just trust that I'm looking out for him but then I fail to listen to a prompting from my Father in Heaven. Or when I complain about him watching other kids play with toys on YouTube and yet I watch other adults buy houses on HGTV.

There are so many incredibly humbling experiences to be had when you become a parent, but when you see your child act just like you, it's pretty much the piece de resistance of parenting. They can give you a much-needed sense of humility and perspective when it comes to dealing with frustrating situations.

Honestly, you can't yell at your kids and then get mad when they yell at you. You can't speak rudely to or about the people around you then get surprised when your kids do the same. You can't be judgmental and be surprised when your kids have the same attitude. You can't be negative about everything you own, then get on your kids for acting entitled.

I don't write any of that with the intention of making you feel guilty! Not at all. We all do it. We all fall short. I know this very well – if I judged you for it, I'd be an even worse hypocrite than I'm already admitting to. What it comes down to is apologizing when necessary and trying to do better.

The most important lesson we can all learn here is the importance of leading by example. Think about it: when someone gives you advice that they don't follow themselves, how likely are you to actually follow that advice? Not very likely, I would imagine. You would immediately write them off as not knowing what they're talking about, and for good reason.

For better or worse, your kids are watching everything you do. They're excellent imitators. When you're kind, when you're rude, when you're merciful, when you're hypocritical – no matter what, they are always looking at you to learn how they should be. How they should talk, look, think, act, and treat others.

As overwhelming as that can feel, that knowledge doesn't need to stress you out you. The good news is, you are under no obligation to be perfect. You're human, and so are your kids. They don't need a perfect role model in you. That wouldn't be relatable, after all — and they have a Savior they can look to as their perfect role model.

As their mother, on the other hand, you can teach them how to handle that imperfection. They can look to you to find out how to act after they've made a mistake. You can model repentance. When you make a mistake with them, you can apologize and ask for a do-over. When you forget to do something that was important to them or your husband, you can apologize and ask how you can make it up to them. You can make sure to keep your promises — and if there comes a time that promise can't be kept, you can choose to own up to it and do what you can to make things right.

Most importantly, you can model what it looks like to be a good, honest, and trustworthy person who lives a Christlike life. You can teach them how to pray through what they see you do. You can teach them how to trust God through trusting Him yourself. You can teach them how to serve by taking care of the least of these whenever possible.

You don't have to preach the gospel day-in and day-out to have a gospel-centered home. In fact, the most powerful preaching you could ever do is by living a Christlike life, not talking about it. If you do the things God most wants you to do and be honest with your kids about it, they'll see how they can do the same for themselves. That's an extremely powerful thing. Don't ever underestimate your influence in their lives.

By being a positive example to your kids, you will have a more powerful impact on them than through anything you could ever say. Your actions speak far louder than words, especially when it comes to your children. Taking that responsibility to heart could be the most powerful decision you make today.

PRAYER IDEAS

- Express gratitude for the opportunity to lead your children by example.
- Ask for help in taking responsibility for that – to try better and give yourself grace as you try to be better.
- Pray to know what you're lacking and for the help you need to work on fixing it.
- Pray to be the example your children need you to be.

FIND YOUR TRIBE

Two are better than one, because they have a good return for their labor:
If either of them falls down, one can help the other up.
But pity anyone who falls and has no one to help them up.
Ecclesiastes 4:9-10

One thing I underestimated about being a mother is how important the village becomes. After all, I'm very much an introvert. I love my friends and family. I love spending time with them, but I'm someone for whom alone time is not optional. It's a requirement to my mental health. And that time with friends and family? It's best one-on-one for me. I don't love crowds.

Of course, I had always heard the old adage, "it takes a village to raise a child." I took it with a grain of salt (as with many of the warnings I heard pre-children), and didn't give much thought to developing that village. I figured the friends I knew at that time would be enough, and didn't need to worry too much about making "mom friends".

However, when I was faced with the reality of being at home, alone, with my sweet baby boy for hours on end, I was forced to realize how boring it could become. Not just boring, though: continuously alternating between mind-numbingly boring and completely overwhelming.

Being a stay-at-home mom is a blessing, no doubt, but the feeling of complete isolation was hard to take. Being alone made me feel like I was doing something wrong. It made me unsure about the decisions I was making and whether they were good enough. I constantly fretted about being enough for my son and my husband, and wasn't sure how to make it all happen.

Most of all, I realized I had completely changed from my pre-child days. From my personality, to my priorities, to my body, everything was so different. I could recognize that, but I had not yet figured out who that new person was. How could I expect my friends to figure that out, too?

While the friends I had at the time were wonderful and did their best to be supportive and understanding, they had no real idea of what I was dealing with emotionally. I really needed the support of other moms to help me figure out what was going on. To help me understand that this was a phase, that it would pass, and that I would get back to my new normal before too long.

I can now say, without a doubt, that it really does take a village to raise a child. Bringing up tiny humans is insanely hard. Arguably the hardest job in the world – though it does have the benefit over law enforcement that you probably won't get shot by the people for whom you're responsible. But seriously, in terms of mental taxation and never-ending-ness, parenthood takes the cake.

Maybe you're lucky and have a village in the form of a church or your husband's department. Maybe you have friends who are sympathetic and understanding. Maybe you don't have any of those things and you're trying to figure out how to fix that. In any case, especially as a solo parent, you definitely need day-in and day-out support.

With that being said, how can you make that happen?

First of all, if you're like me and tend toward introversion, you'll have to start by being willing to put yourself out there. It can feel awkward, but when you're at the park with your kids, try to interact with other moms. If your kids hit it off with other kids, introduce yourself to their mom. If you hit it off, ask to plan a playdate.

Yes, it can feel super awkward, no doubt. Sometimes it feels like you're back in the dating scene again and asking someone on a date. It's all good. When it comes down to it, someone has to be willing to put themselves out there. Take the risk and be willing to let that person be you.

Side note: Be careful not to write anyone off on first impressions. I've been tempted to do this, and been so glad for a second (or third) opportunity to get to know them — some of those very people have ended up being my very best friends! If I'd stuck to my initial impression, I would have greatly missed out.

Second of all, look for opportunities to meet other people. I know it can be easier to stay at home with your kids, rather than get them dressed, ready, and out the door, but doing that guarantees you'll never meet new friends.

If you're not sure where to start, I would suggest checking out your local library or recreation center to see if they have any free events for kids. Not only does that give you a fun thing to do with the kids, but it also gives you the opportunity to find likeminded families who enjoy the same kinds of things.

Third, even though it can be hard to ask for help, make sure that you do. I know that I have a hard time with this, personally. I tend to burn the candle at both ends and get to complete burnout before asking for help, and it's not good. There are times I've been burned out and asking for help kind of made me feel like a failure, but I know in my heart that's not the case.

I mean, I would be happy to help another woman who needed it without thinking for even a second that she was a failure. Yet, I have a hard time extending that same logic to myself. Regardless, there are a lot of people who love us and our children and would love to help us so we can parent better.

Trust me, when my son is out of the house for a few hours hanging out with friends, he comes back and it's like a totally new relationship. I'm more patient with his shortcomings and he's more willing to listen and obey. It causes much more harmony than if we're around each other nonstop 24/7.

If you are scared to ask for help because you are worried someone's going to judge you, don't be worried about that! Nobody is going to judge you – and if they do, they're not worth your time anyway because they're jerks. In all seriousness, though, we all need a little help sometimes to be the best parents we can be.

Lastly, sometimes getting creative can help you get the support you need. I personally joined a gym recently to get a daily 90-minute break from parenting. Honestly, the workout is secondary to the break I get – I'll end up getting in shape as a matter of consequence, I think. But the money spent each month is worth every penny to make sure I'm mentally taken care enough to be a good mom to my kids.

You can also trade childcare with other mom friends at times. Especially as your kids get older, it becomes mutually beneficial – because rather than childcare, it ends up being a much-needed break on both ends, because the kids entertain each other. Win-win!

You've got this – but never underestimate how much friends can help you be so much better.

PRAYER IDEAS

- Express gratitude for the friends and family you have that support you.
- Ask for help in nurturing those existing support systems.
- Pray to find likeminded people who will understand you and support you – the women who will make up your tribe.
- Pray to discern what others need from you, and the opportunity to bless them with those things.
- Pray for courage to seek help when you need it and give yourself grace for not being able to do it all yourself.

PEACEFUL HOME

My people will live in peaceful dwelling places,
in secure homes, in undisturbed places of rest.
Isaiah 32:18

So far in this devotional, we've covered making you, your parenting, and your marriage more peaceful. Of course, none of these things exists all by themselves. They all impact each other. Heck, you know this. When you're feeling lousy, your parenting and wifely duties tend to be done with less joy. When parenting is tough, it takes it out of you. When you and your husband are fighting, you tend to be snippier with the kids. I get it!

With that in mind, it's now time to bring all the things we have been talking about together to make sure the environment of your home is the most peaceful it can be. This is where we focus our efforts specifically on making your home the refuge it deserves to be – the refuge that will allow you all to live a life that is in the world, but not of the world.

Whether or not you believe in "hauntings", per se, there's no doubt that homes can have a spirit about them. There are some homes that set you at ease the moment you walk into them. Others make you cringe for one reason or another – sometimes it's for obvious reasons (like, say, drug paraphernalia), sometimes it's just an unspecific feeling you get.

Some of those feelings comes down to things that are out of your control, like the actual physical layout of your home or the time and energy you have to put into things like decorating (or vacuuming – as I write this, I can't totally remember the last time I vacuumed.) Others are the safe, happy, loving feelings that you focus on trying to cultivate, rather than focusing on the negative. That's what this chapter focuses on, because they are what you have the most control over, and they're the most important.

As a law enforcement family, the reality is that the negativity of the world has more of an impact on your family life. Your husband especially can't help but be affected. The things he sees when he's protecting and serving are not easily forgotten when he returns home from his shift. They remain on his heart and mind, and can weigh him down day after day.

While this isn't something you can protect him from completely, you can be take care of the spirit of your home. To ensure that your home is a safe, welcoming place to be. The first three sections were a good introduction to this, but now we'll go deeper into making sure the good influences within your house can overcome the negative impact of law enforcement life.

Maybe that seems like a huge task. Maybe when it comes down to it, you're not even sure if that kind of peacefulness is possible. Maybe you feel like the best you can hope for is simple survival, nothing more.

If that is the case, take heart. Know that God can overcome all evil for you, your husband, and your family. He loves you all. He knows the things your husband faces every single day, whether anyone else knows or understands it or not. He understands his struggles perfectly.

He understands your struggles perfectly. He understands the struggles of your husband and children perfectly. Trust me when I say that He has a special place in His heart for all of you, and He will not leave you to fend for yourselves.

What it comes down to is intentionally making time for God in your home. It means protecting your home from negative influences as much as possible.

That is what this chapter is all about.

SECTIONS

- People Over Things
- In The World, Not Of The World
- Love One Another
- Being Unified in Christ
- Staying Connected

PEOPLE OVER THINGS

Store up for yourselves treasures in heaven,
where moths and vermin do not destroy,
and where thieves do not break in and steal.
For where your treasure is, there your heart will be also.

Matthew 6:20-21

Doesn't it just break your heart when you hear of tsunamis, wildfires, hurricanes, or some other natural disaster that drives people from their homes? There are so many of these stories in the news, where people lose everything they have ever known because of a natural disaster.

With these news reports come the pictures of homes reduced to nothing in the aftermath. Sometimes it's impossible to believe they were actual dwelling places prior to the disaster. To think of every personal belonging, all treasured objects, family heirlooms, every beloved toy being absolutely destroyed. Gone, sometimes literally overnight.

Truthfully, it's unthinkable. I suppose there's a reason for the phrase, "You don't know what you've got until it's gone." It's easy to take the things you have every day for granted until those things aren't there anymore.

But, of course, these things do happen. Because they do, it forces you to think: what would life be like if you lost everything tomorrow? If everything you had worked so hard to build in your life – that is, all material things – were completely gone, and all you had left was your family?

While I'm sure it would be devastating to have those things go missing in one fell swoop, it's the old cliché where I'm sure you would end up saying, "At least we're all safe." In light of everything you have lost, you would cling to one another that much more – especially in a disaster that also caused loss of life, having your family intact would make the loss of all the stuff no longer important.

When I face these questions in my everyday life, they bring to mind the leading scripture of this section. Is my heart on the things of the world, or the things of God? The things of the world are short-lived and easily taken – by thieves, moths, vermin, disaster – but the things of God are forever.

Your family, as such, is the greatest treasure God could provide to you. That's why it's so important to remember to place people over things at all times, in all things, and in all places – because the people in your life are irreplaceable.

Time isn't guaranteed. The future isn't guaranteed. No one knows what tomorrow, or even the next hour, holds. That is exactly why it's so important to make sure you treasure the people with whom you share your life more than any material possession.

After all, I have never, ever heard of anyone on their deathbed wishing they had bought a more expensive sofa. That they had bought that must-have video game. That they had had a bigger house they could better brag to their friends about. Rather, when disaster comes and the reality of death comes calling, people by far wish they had spent more time with the people they love most.

It can be all too easy to lose sight of this truth, however. There is always something new and awesome being advertised to you. It's the advertiser's job to make you believe it is "the thing" that will finally bring you happiness, above all other things. Even I get trapped in the, "once I get (fill in the blank here), then I'll be happy." The world spends a lot of time trying to convince you of that very thing, when really, joy comes from loving others.

Sometimes it isn't even stuff that distracts us from our family, but tasks we need to accomplish. Whether we get distracted by home projects, everyday chores, work tasks, weight loss, or some other pursuit, the fact remains that any of these things can inadvertently take precedence over the relationships you have with your family. Even though many of those things are good (even necessary!) to your everyday well-being, taking it to the extreme isn't good, either.

The truth is, none of us has enough time for all the things we would like to do. We all have the same constraint: a 24-hour day in which we need at least some sleep. Laying up your treasure in heaven means using that time carefully to build up what matters most – and that means focusing on what lasts the longest.

Sometimes that means when your family is at odds with one another for whatever reason, sometimes it's okay to drop what you're doing to feed your relationships. Your dishes can wait another day or two, but your family is constantly changing and growing, and you all need one another to help shape each other into who you need to become.

There's no denying it: this life can be incredibly hard. This life is filled with pain, fear, and uncertainty, and that will be the case pretty much until Christ comes again. When you prioritize time together as a family as much as possible, it means you are helping one another face the scary, uncertain world together. Everyone in your family knows they have people who love and support them, no matter what happens. That can make the hardest burdens far easier to bear.

By always making sure your family keeps a "people over things" kind of attitude, you can make sure you make the most of every minute and have no regrets if something bad were to happen to anyone in your family. Laying up your treasure in Heaven and in the special family relationships God has provided to you means you can truly live without fear of the future.

No matter what comes your way, make sure the people in your life comes over any material possession, any reward, any accolade, any pridefulness, any *anything*, because you never know when it could just be too late. Live today to the fullest, and you will all be as happy as possible.

PRAYER IDEAS

- Express gratitude for the people who make up your family and circle of friends, and for everyone He has brought into your life.
- Thank God for providing you with the things you need to live comfortably.
- Thank God for providing for you and your family emotionally.
- Ask for help making sure the people in your family always come before the things of the world.
- Ask for help meeting the emotional needs of your family, especially those they aren't able to verbalize/ask for.

IN THE WORLD, NOT OF THE WORLD

My prayer is not that you take them out of the world
but that you protect them from the evil one.
They are not of the world, even as I am not of it.
John 17:15-16

With my husband's knowledge of the world outside our Christian community, we sometimes find ourselves a little at odds with others who don't have the same experiences. It's not that either of us has bad intentions or anything, just that we have had opportunities to view the world differently than they have.

Some others within our church have such limited interactions with others that they believe other people are generally good. They don't understand the reality of drug addiction, child abuse, violent crimes, or any of the horrendous things we unfortunately know all too much about.

When they hear about those things, they tend to think they are isolated incidents, or that they're the fault of someone else, that nobody would possibly choose those things. They don't see the bad stuff that often, so they don't realize how prevalent it actually is. The men and women of law enforcement, for better or worse, don't have that luxury.

It's been the cause of many discussions between myself and my husband, both about general worldviews and in the decisions we make because of it. For instance, we almost never give money to panhandlers, unless the spirit moves us otherwise. Sometimes that means we're seen as a little heartless, but it's because we know the truth. Does it mean we're not willing to help? No way. Just that we know it's usually not a legit cry for help.

Knowing the evils of the world allows us to be more discerning. For example, my husband's knowledge of drugs, which I always joke is just shy of a that of an addict's, has helped him immensely in law enforcement in the past. It's helped him recognize signs and symptoms of particular drugs. It has helped him save lives that may otherwise have been lost. If he didn't know of the things of the world, he wouldn't know how to do that.

Similarly, that means we need to be as honest as possible with our children about the things they will encounter. There is no end to the ways in which the world can undermine and attack what is most important to God, and the things that your family values the most. That means your family needs to be prepared, especially when these attacks come as unfortunate surprises.

As much as you would like to be forewarned of your children's exposure to negative influences, you don't always have that luxury. For instance, neighbors of ours told us that they had to unfortunately give an impromptu "birds and the bees" talk to their son after they bought a secondhand truck that had pornographic DVDs in the bed — and they didn't realize it until their 8 year old came to ask them about what he had found.

Of course, it's a talk every parent prepares for, but having to do so in such a "jumping in the deep end" way was tough. That's just one example of many, really, of how the world can try to worm its way into your home. Other ways include the things that pop up on your

Facebook or Instagram feed, or commercials that come on when you're watching otherwise family-friendly shows, or just people you encounter on the street.

The way this impacts your family depends on your family, its values, and of course the threat you're up against, but there's no denying that there is no way to completely shield your kids from the world. The good news, though, is that you don't have to.

After all, Christ asked us to be in the world, but not of the world. Shielding each other from the ugliness of the world does you and your children a disservice. If they don't know the things of the world, if they don't know if or why they are bad, those things don't always seem so bad. Satan works in lots of different ways to make certain things not seem as bad as they are – in fact to make them seem more loving and caring than God's way of doing things.

That's not to say that your kids need to know everything all at once, but introducing them to the idea of good pictures and bad pictures, for instance, can help open the dialogue about pornography before they're even at an age where it can become an issue. Talking about drugs and alcohol and their effects, without being too graphic, can help you talk about those things more openly before peer pressure even comes into play.

The way I see this is that sometimes people will accuse Christians of trying to raise your children in a bubble. Sometimes our faith in Christ is seen as a shield, making us not see the bad things in the world. But that isn't the case. After all, Christ experienced everything we would ever experience. He knows our pains perfectly – none of the ugliness of the world is a secret to him.

Rather than raising children in a protective bubble, you can think of it as nurturing them in a greenhouse. They are safe and protected from the things that will not nourish them, but the things that will help them grow best are magnified. You can filter things as necessary to help them grow properly, giving them only as much information as is needed to keep themselves safe.

It's important that you as a family are honest, upfront, and forthright with one another about the evil in the world. You have to understand what you're going to face as you venture out, but be careful not to entertain it. As the scriptures say, guard your heart, for everything you do flows from it.

This means that to know of the world, you obviously don't need to experiment with those things. If you know the destructive effect of influences of the world, you can see them from afar without having to experience them firsthand.

Likewise, if you and your husband have made serious mistakes in the past, those things might be worth discussing with your kids — as age-appropriate, of course. After all, if you were walking with your children in the forest and tripped over a branch, would you allow them to trip over the same thing to save face? No, you would point it out and help them avoid the same mistake as yourself.

To limit the effect of potential destructive influences in your home, you have to be able to identify them. To know your enemy is to be able to eradicate and defeat your enemy, whatever you currently define that enemy as. Being honest, upfront, and forthright in everything with your family can help give them the power they need to be in the world, but not of the world.

PRAYER IDEAS

- Thank God for allowing you to be in the world, not of the world – to be protected from the Evil One, as Christ's prayer discusses.
- Express gratitude for both the seen and unseen ways God keeps you and your family safe from evil.
- Ask for help approaching difficult topics with your children in ways that will inform them of danger without scaring them.
- Ask for ways in which you can resist temptation to be more like the world, and help your family do the same.

LOVE ONE ANOTHER

A new command I give you: Love one another.
As I have loved you, so you must love one another.
John 13:34

My husband and I are very different in how we want to be shown love. Personally, I feel extremely loved when he acknowledges the things I do and helps me with them. I love when he tells me how proud he is of me – it makes my heart feel all warm and fuzzy, and makes me happier for the rest of the day.

Meanwhile, he loves when I snuggle, hold his hand, and spend good, focused time with him without being distracted by kids, work, or electronics. It doesn't happen nearly as often as I would like, admittedly, but at least I know this about him – one step in the right direction, right?

Similarly, our kids need different things from us. Honestly, our youngest is just a baby, so all she really wants is milk and attention. It's easily done, since she's so cute and smiley all the time. Our oldest thrives on active, silly play – which can sometimes be a tall order when he has two introverted parents who aren't inherently active and silly, but we both see how happy he is when we overcome our reservations and join in his games.

The point is, love can be expressed in so many different ways. You can write notes or praise others in person. You can hug and kiss them. You can encourage them when they're feeling down. You can play with them or draw pictures with them. You can bake them a treat or make their favorite dinner. You can send them funny memes when they're having a hard day.

However you choose to show love, no matter how the people around you receive it best, what matters most is that God wants all His children to love one another. There is nowhere that commandment is more important than in your own home, with your own husband and children.

All of you have been brought together on this earth for a reason. There are things you can learn from one another. There are things you need from one another. Possibly the most important thing we need from those we're closest to is their unconditional love through everything life throws at us.

Love within your family home can help each of you overcome the worst of trials. It can uplift you and help you find courage when you're faced with hard decisions. It can make the ugliness of the world a lot less ugly – or, at least, a lot less impactful to your psyche, because you can witness it from afar instead of personally.

Sometimes, though, loving those closest to you can be a hard thing to do. I'll confess that I sometimes find it easier to do nice things for strangers than the people I spend every day with. I mean, don't get me wrong. I always and forever love my family with all my heart, but being together day in and day out, we also have more space to frustrate each other on a more personal level.

Sometimes the people you spend so much time with become experts on what pushes your buttons – whether intentionally or not. Sometimes it's your husband who leaves his gear all over the bathroom counter – again. Sometimes it's your child, the born engineer, who's always asking, "What happens if I do this?" and all too often, the answer is you cleaning up a sticky, ridiculous mess that makes you crabby. Been there.

However, maybe the fact that it can be harder is exactly why it's that much more important. You see each other at your best and at your worst – your completely unvarnished, true selves. The love shown under that circumstance is the truest love of all, when you think about it.

Whatever the case, there is one thing for certain. Love is about spending time on the people that matter most. It's about meeting their needs in the way they need you to meet them. It's about paying attention to what they need most and doing what you can to fulfill that need. That results in them feeling happy, safe, loved, appreciated, and like they truly belong where they are.

Serve one another as much as possible. When your husband or your kids need your help, do what you can to help them joyfully (without groaning about how frustrated you are – no, really, I get it!) Doing that service with a joy-filled heart is going to make it that much more effective, and not just for them. It will make you happier about it too!

Do what you can to help keep the peace in your household. When you sense there is a disagreement or a lapse in understanding between members of your beloved family, try to bridge the gap. Sometimes an outside perspective is all that's needed to help two people find common ground in an argument, and I can say for sure I play peacemaker a lot between my son and daughter, and between the kids and their dad. I know each of them better than the other does, so I can help give insight to what each of them was thinking and feeling when making their decisions or saying what they said.

Be gentle and forgiving in every circumstance possible, and encourage your family members to do the same. Modeling it is a great start, but you can also verbally encourage them to take it easy on one another. You can help them understand others, even those outside your family, by trying to give them perspective of what they might be going through that made them act in such a hurtful way. You can take a breath before responding to something frustrating, and decide to say something in a kinder way – to find a solution rather than trying to place blame.

Pray for one another, and with one another, as often as possible – or at least once a day! This simple action will bring you closer together as a family than almost any other decision you could make. Hearing each other pray for one another, especially when you do so by name, is the most amazing thing – it can soften your heart toward one another and help you realize that you are truly loved. And, vice versa, help those you love know how much you truly love them, and how you are always looking out for them.

The other day, my son randomly announced, "Jesus said we have to be nice to people." I was a little surprised, turned down my music, and said, "Yeah, you're right, buddy." And in that phrase, he pretty much nailed Jesus's greatest commandment to us – because he specifically said, just as He loved us, we must love one another – no matter what.

To truly show love to one another, we have to take action. These are the actions that will help you show how much you truly love those you treasure most in your life, and they will make your whole family happier for it.

PRAYER IDEAS

- Express gratitude to God for the wonderful family He has given you.
- Express to Him how much you love your family and why (He knows this, but trust me – verbalizing it just makes those feelings grow!)
- Ask for guidance on loving your family in the ways they need and desire it most.
- Ask for help filling your own cup so you can help meet their needs emotionally.
- Ask that your family can see what you need and help to meet those needs as well.
- Ask for opportunities to show your family how much you love them.

BEING UNIFIED IN CHRIST

There is one body, but it has many parts.
But all its many parts make up one body.
It is the same with Christ.
Corinthians 12:12

When I was a teenager, I have to admit: I was incredibly jealous of my sister. I'm sure it's not an unfamiliar story, but I felt like she was so perfect. She got good grades in school, which to me seemed like it was effortless for her. She was (is, really) an amazing singer, enough to get into school for vocal performance. She was good in sports. She made friends easily, and was very sociable. She always seemed to know the right thing to say in conversations. I always believed my parents preferred her to me.

After all, I could study my buns off and still pull a C in math. It just didn't click, no matter how hard I tried. Sports? Ha. I relate well to Pam in The Office when she says, "Here's my high school gym, where I pretended to have PMS to avoid everything." Roughly paraphrased, but you get the picture. And social? Again, *ha*. I'm a socially awkward introvert who's more comfortable greeting pets at a party than the people there.

These are things that I have always felt insecure about. When I compared myself to my brother and sister, I felt I had gotten the short end of the stick. Why couldn't I be the pretty, popular one everyone seemed to like?

The thing is, focusing on those things that I wasn't good at made me miss the things I *was* good at. Even though I'm not "good" at social situations, per se, I am good at helping people who need it. My issue is I hate small talk — but skip the small talk and get to something that really matters, and we're gold.

Likewise, all that math and science I killed myself to learn? I remember precisely nothing about it. I've always been good in my English classes, though, as I loved reading and writing — but I always wrote it off as not that important because it wasn't what people admired my siblings for. Now, guess what? I write for a living.

My point is, in all my discomfort with myself, I missed out on identifying the things that made me special. My shortcomings, as I saw them, weren't really shortcomings except for in particular situations. However, when you think about it, that same thing applies to a fish's ability to swim or a bird's ability to fly — not good for all situations, but pretty darn amazing all the same.

The truth is, I am just fine the way I am, because God made me this way for a reason. The same is true for you. He knew the things you would face in your life. He knew the things you would need, and the things the people around you would need, and gave you talents (and opportunities to develop those talents) to help you meet those needs.

After all, we are compared to parts of the body of Christ.[1] Think of all the different parts of your body. You have hands, eyes, ears, kidneys, lungs, an appendix... okay, maybe that last one is a bad

---

[1] 1 Corinthians 12:12-27

example. But all the parts of your body work together to do what you need it to do.

Heck, think of the intricacy of just your eye, and that's just one relatively small part of your body. It has lenses, nerves, rods, cones, and all sorts of things that, most of the time, just work, without you having to do anything special to make it work.

A body can't just be made of one part. If you had a body made of eyes, you wouldn't be able to hear, walk, or do anything. Plus, honestly, it sounds like the plot of a really bad 80's horror film. But truly, you have so many different parts of your body that all need to be different.

The special gifts and talents God gives each of us are designed to help us make the world a better place. What you are jealous of in someone else isn't really all that important to you. It's okay to be different. Why should a heart be jealous of a brain, when neither can survive without the other?

Morbid mental imagery aside, I'm sure you have both talents you're proud of and shortcomings you are ashamed of. What if you could embrace those and realize they are all part of God's amazing design for your life? They're there to make you, your family, and the world a better place. The different skills we all have are part of the grand design for the Body of Christ.

The beauty of this is, we don't have to compare ourselves to others and feel bad about the stuff we can't do. We're not supposed to be able to do everything all by ourselves. We are supposed to work in concert with others to accomplish everything God wants us to do.

Isn't that freeing? I know that knowledge makes me feel really warm and fuzzy toward Heavenly Father for making me as I am, in His ultimate wisdom.

What's amazing is His plan doesn't end there. He made me different from my husband, and our children different from each other. Yet, we all make up one family unit — one unit of people who can be unified in Christ to do amazing things for Him and make the world a better place.

You can take advantage of this knowledge by making sure you magnify one another's gifts and talents. Recognize what each of you is good at. Compliment one another for your uniqueness. The things you struggle with about each other, try to find the benefits to them.

Don't neglect to actually use your talents. Find opportunities to use them and to strengthen them in everyday life. Pray for those opportunities and take advantage of them when they come up, as they inevitably will.

Discouragement will come. It's only human nature to wish you could be a little more of "something", and it doesn't help that Satan wants nothing more than to bring you down so you don't reach your full potential. Know that those times will come, but put your trust in God anyway. Realize that through you, the power of God can do amazing works for good.

In the end, each member of your family is different — and no matter how much strife that can cause, it's with a glorious purpose in mind. With God's help, you can become closer to one another, work together more efficiently, and truly work as the body of Christ.

PRAYER IDEAS

- Express gratitude for the unique way God has made you, acknowledging that it was done according to His wisdom.
- Thank God for every gift and talent He has given you.
- Thank God for the different gifts and talents each member of your family has, acknowledging that you all get to benefit from one another's.
- Ask for help identifying your individual gifts and talents, especially when you aren't feeling so special.
- Ask for help nurturing the gifts and talents of your family, especially in your children.

STAYING CONNECTED

How good and pleasant it is when God's people live together in unity!
Psalm 133:1

I take some pride in the fact that at least 60% of the time, I feel like I have things covered at home so my husband doesn't need to worry about them. Sure, it's not 100% of the time – not even close, really – but all things considered, I think it's an accomplishment worthy of feeling proud of.

Of course, that comes with downsides. Sometimes I get so used to doing things on my own that I forget to communicate about things that affect both myself and my husband. Things like discipline issues with the kids, decisions about attending family events, even the existence of those events at times, or decisions on how to spend money.

While I like that I feel capable of doing those things on my own, it's understandable that my DIY abilities make him feel a little superfluous when he comes back home. It makes him feel like he's just another chess piece I need to move around, and he doesn't feel all that good about it.

The downside of feeling capable of doing things like that on my own is definitely something I have to work on, all the time – I need to constantly keep myself in check to make sure I'm keeping my husband in the loop, and not just making all the decisions we should be making as a couple all by myself.

Beyond just decision-making, though, I sometimes find myself forgetting to send him updates about the kids. I fail to send the good moments we have together, so he sometimes just gets a long string of me complaining about how hard my day is — which doesn't always make his day much better. Or, should I say, pretty much always makes his day harder.

Whether you're the same way or you struggle more with staying up on all the things you need to do, focusing on helping your family to stay connected with one another is incredibly important — not just to each of your individual well-being, but also to the health of your marriage and the emotional well-being of your children.

With all the demands on your husband's time and energy, and yours, as a law enforcement family, it can be hard to really stay connected. I mean, you have the house to keep track of, the kids and their schooling, plus possibly a job (or two) on the side, maybe even for both of you. Your husband has a demanding, unpredictable schedule that comes with a huge emotional load. Your kids have school, friends, and their own growing-up issues.

Even though those things present barriers to staying connected, they make doing so that much more important. Uniting as a team through everything means neither of you has to feel like you're going it alone. Your husband gets to know that he can depend on his family to be there for him after even the worst shifts. You get to know that you're appreciated for all you do to make everything else work. Your kids get to know they have both of you to depend on in the hardest trials they face.

It's going to make you all stronger as a family and as individuals. It's going to make it so you can support each other through any and all trials, no matter how awful life can get. It's going to give you a strong foundation on which to build the rest of your life. It's going to allow you to come closer to God – all of you – because it will help you feel peaceful and in a place to hear His word.

Maybe more importantly, it will help give you a group of people on whom you can fall back on, who can not only support you through the hard times of life, who can rally around you, but can also be trusted to point you to God when you need to be pointed to Him. And you can point them to Him, as well.

The truth is, you all need each other so much. Families are forever, and God loves you all so much. He loves you enough that He gave you one another to abide with: to learn from, to get support from, and generally to enjoy as you walk through this life.

How can you stay connected when law enforcement life tends to preclude that kind of close, consistent, family connection? Trust me when I say it is not impossible. It really just requires consistency – love, communication, and appreciation of one another's unique personalities.

When it comes down to it, it is mostly about doing the little things you can do every day. Things like leaving notes for each other, texting to let people know you were thinking about them, bridging the gap between people when they're misunderstanding one another, and trying to understand where others are coming from without overreacting and getting upset.

You can also use cell phones for a lot of good. Sure, they can be a force of distraction, too, but when used wisely, they are a good way to connect with your family and vice versa. Sending texts, photos, videos, and even using apps like Marco Polo lets share in one another's days, no matter how crazy your days become. No matter what shift the department has your officer working. No matter what your kids homework load looks like.

They even have Facebook Messenger for kids now, plus a myriad of ways to provide your kids the benefits of a smartphone without the huge number of dangers that can come with them. The digital age can be disconnecting if used incorrectly, but when used for its intended purpose, it can help your family become stronger and happier, every day.

Take the opportunity to connect in everything you do – whether it's getting up and ready for the day, or making dinner, or driving to school or work, you can make it an opportunity to connect no matter what.

Staying connected means you will all be happier, and is completely worth the effort.

PRAYER IDEAS

- Express gratitude for the opportunities you have to spend time with your family.
- Thank Him for the ways he helps your family come together as one, to live together in unity.
- Ask for help making sure you stay connected to your family, especially when you feel there is a lapse.
- Ask what you can do to close any emotional gaps between yourself and members of your family.

FINAL THOUGHTS

The rain came down, the streams rose, and the winds blew and beat against that house; yet it did not fall, because it had its foundation on the rock.
Matthew 7:25

You are pretty wonderful, you know that? I'm so happy you've read through this devotional, because it tells me that having a happy home is something really important to you. It's a goal that matters to you. That tells me that you are going to do wonderful things – you know, not that you haven't already!

That being said, when you're working toward a goal, it's normal to get discouraged at times – especially when it's a big one. Working toward a more peaceful home for you, your officer, and your children is not going to happen overnight. You can't fix every shortcoming through reading one devotional, one time.

The good news about that, though, is that nobody expects you to be perfect! You are just fine being the world's okayest wife, mom, police wife – everything. God absolutely *loves* you just the way you are. That means you can free yourself from being perfect right this minute, and rely on Him to help you get to where you would ultimately like to be.

Every day, you can make small choices that lead you closer to that goal. You can choose small things to improve yourself as a mother, as a wife, in your calling, or to help your family come closer together. Long-term goals are achieved not through quick sprints, but small, consistent efforts over time.

If you feel overwhelmed thinking of all the changes you would like to make, take heart. Nobody is expecting you to do it all. And, of course, nobody expects you to do it all by yourself. You can make it a goal as a family to be closer, more peaceful, and happier. You can encourage your husband and children in making better decisions.

Best of all, you and your family can partner with the One who knows you best. The One who can and will help you through every storm. By devoting your life to Christ and helping your family do the same, you build the foundation of your home on his rock – the only strong, unshakeable foundation you can rely on.

God never fails. You may fail at times. No, let me rephrase: you *will* fail at times, and so will those you love most. The God you worship, however, will never fail you. He is always there, always ready to hear your prayers, no matter how feeble they may seem. His power is perfect.

With that knowledge, you can go forth in confidence. You don't have to fret about the ways you fall short. We all do that, trust me! It doesn't make you less worthy in any way.

Going forward, what you focus on is completely up to you. Depending on what section has resonated with you while reading, you might decide to focus on getting yourself some more alone time so you can build yourself up. You might choose to focus on your hobbies, so you have more emotional energy to spend on your family.

Maybe you struggle more with parenting, especially if you have a specific challenge with one (or more) of your children right now. Maybe it feels like the time to feed those relationships more than others.

Hey, maybe your relationship with your husband is what you're currently struggling with for whatever reason. You might choose to focus on those chapters relating to marriage, and prayerfully decide what you need to focus on to make yourself and your officer happier as a couple.

Whatever the case may be, do what you feel is right for yourself and your family. This guide is just that — a starting point to the greatest adventure God has to offer you, which is building up your family: Getting to know your spouse and become even more one flesh. Raising your children in a Godly way, a way that will help them change the world one day. Devoting your own time and talents to worthy causes that themselves change the world.

It's the best adventure of your life, and I hope you treasure every moment you get.

ACKNOWLEDGEMENTS

I'm so grateful for all the help I have received in writing this book. My husband, of course, for being my biggest supporter. Even when he doesn't totally understand my vision for the projects I'm working on, he supports me 100%. I have to thank my kids for being wonderful inspirations and sources of helping me become a better person. They get me out of my comfort zone every day, and I know they're teaching me way more than I'm teaching them.

I'm grateful for our sitter, Riley, who has been so flexible and accommodating as I try to arrange our schedules and try to get my work done while she hangs out with the kiddos. Thanks for being a listening ear on the rare occasion they fall asleep at the same time, and for facilitating some much-needed date nights. You are the best!

I have to express a huge thank you to Erin, my editor, who took the time to comb through the drafts of this book, making sure I got my point across clearly. I also have to apologize for the time I accidentally sent her part I had written with one hand while nursing. Points to her for still trying to edit the darn thing, though she did ask if I had written it after a few glasses of wine – I'm sorry for the headache, but thank you for the laugh!

Thank you to the friends and family who have supported me at all times, especially when I started to doubt myself. I could not have done this without you guys.

Most of all, I'm grateful for the opportunity I have to help the wives of those in law enforcement. I know how hard it is, and I'm so grateful I've been put in a position to help make things even a little easier.

God has been so good to me. I'm grateful for the skills and talents He has provided me. I'm grateful for His guiding hand making sure that everything works together for my good. I'm grateful that He never gives up on me, even when I act like a petulant child because I don't understand His plan. I'm grateful for where he has led me and where He continues to lead both me and my family, and I can't wait to see where we go from here.

And you, reader. Thank you, truly, from the bottom of my heart, for giving me the opportunity to help you. Thank you for your never-ending support; I only hope I can give you as much as you have given me!

ABOUT THE AUTHOR

Leah Everly is the blogger behind Love and Blues Blog, where she helps police wives in their often difficult calling. When she's not busy writing, she can usually be found wrangling her kids or snuggled up with her nose in a book. She lives in Salt Lake City with her husband, a former police officer, and their two super-cute children.

If you'd like to follow more of Leah's writings, check her out on loveandbluesblog.com.

COULD YOU DO ME A QUICK FAVOR?

Hi there – Leah here :)

I hope you've enjoyed this devotional!

If that's been the case, would you mind leaving a review of the book on Amazon? It would be a HUGE help to me in getting this book in the hands of those who need it most.

Thank you so much, and have an awesome day!

Love,
Leah

CPSIA information can be obtained
at www.ICGtesting.com
Printed in the USA
LVHW031330141019
634125LV00007B/3176/P